HARWICH
THROUGH TIME

JOAN M. MALONEY &
CAROLE DECHRISTOPHER

AMERICA
THROUGH
TIME

America Through Time®
An imprint of Sutton Publishing Inc.
www.through-time.com

First published 2013
This edition published 2026

ISBN 978-1-63499-615-0

Typeset in Mrs Eaves XL Serif Narrow
Printed and bound in the United States of America

INTRODUCTION

Harwich today is a thriving community of about twenty-two square miles on Lower Cape Cod. Like neighboring towns, the area is particularly attractive as a retirement choice and an attraction to city dwellers seeking a vacation home. Its year round population of about twelve thousand explodes to at least triple that total each summer. How has this happened?

In the beginning, when the first settlers migrated from Plymouth Plantation, there was sandy soil and salty seawater. Small farms, cod fishing and the packet boat trade provided most livelihoods, though sometimes quite precariously. All this changed in the mid 1800s, when farmers realize the profit that could be made by cultivating cranberries. About the same time, the arrival of the railroad meant the death of the packet ship trade and cod fishing by hook was replaced by the more lucrative seining of herring.

From its incorporation as a town in 1694, the seven villages that made up Harwich offered great promise. After the split from Brewster in 1803, the villages began to find their own special niches. By the 1850s, the Center was the mercantile and cultural hub, with its banks, stores, and high school – all clustered in the shadows of the Congregational Church. The effects of the Civil War, however, brought great changes. In times of economic recession and high unemployment the population dwindled: men left in search of work. The prewar total of 3,350 residents would not be matched again until after the First World War.

The sea, that once had provided about two-thirds of all income, was to have its own rebirth in about 1900. The charming beaches, the popularity of automobiles, and the foresight of several local benefactors provided paved roads and fine lodging accommodations that drew even more visitors. Job opportunities rose, as did land values.

The present time represents yet another major stage in the town's evolution. Many a charming old building had survived simply because there were no buyers Now tear downs of these treasures provide space for the new 'MacMansions' – especially along the shore line. Fortunately, residents and summer people have organized to protect open space and land conservation efforts thrive. Amid all this activity, Harwich remembers its past and honors those who went before.

These pages are meant to illustrate both the forces of stability and those of change. Imagine when the 'now' photographs become the 'thens'. You must judge who are the winners and who are the losers.

Acknowledgments

We are grateful to the following for so graciously sharing their photographs (identified by page and placement): Alice Bonatt 42A; Gladys DeChristopher 76A; Adele Geraghty 56A; Joy Hutchins Harrison-Olson 58A; Betty Deane Holmes 74A; Jill Mason 92A; Peapod by Stop & Shop 62b; E.G. Perry, *A Trip Around Cape Cod,* published in 1898 and now in the public domain, 32A and 35A; Suzanne Routhier Postcard Collection 22A, 23A, 28A, 37A, 38A,40A, 44A, 40A,50A 60B, 72A,79A, 80A, 82A; Matt Sutphin, 11B.

All the other old photographs are from the Harwich Historical Society's Collection.

Special appreciation to Emily Lindberg and Jeanette Louth for their gift to the Society of Charles D. Cahoon's painting "Iceboating on Long Pond," included here on page 71.

We are most appreciative of the unfailing help and support of Brooks Academy Museum Director Desiree Mobed.

All the present-day photographs not otherwise identified above were taken by the authors. We, of course, are responsible for any errors

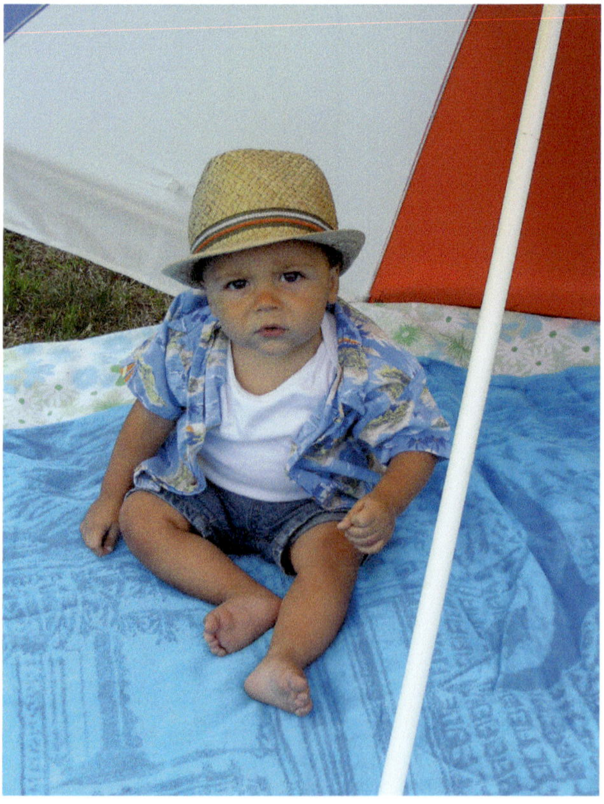

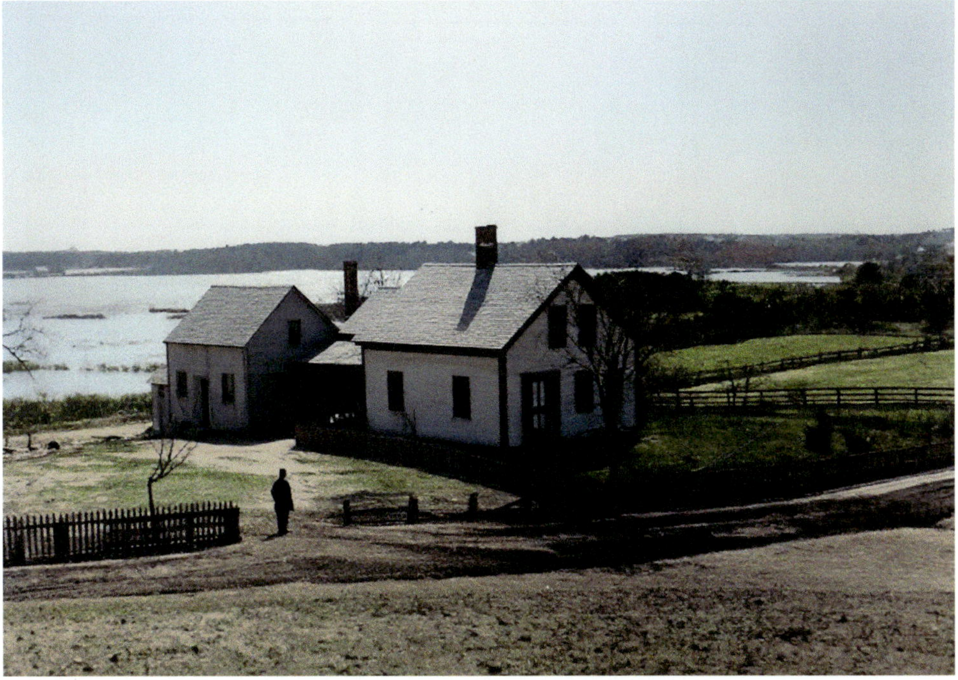

MOODY FARM: Sand dunes and salty air are fine for song lyrics, but not for productive farming. The Samuel Moody farm overlooked Grassy Pond on Bank Street. The farmhouse has been moved to the opposite side of the road and beautifully restored by Dr. Stanson A. Moody, a direct descendent.

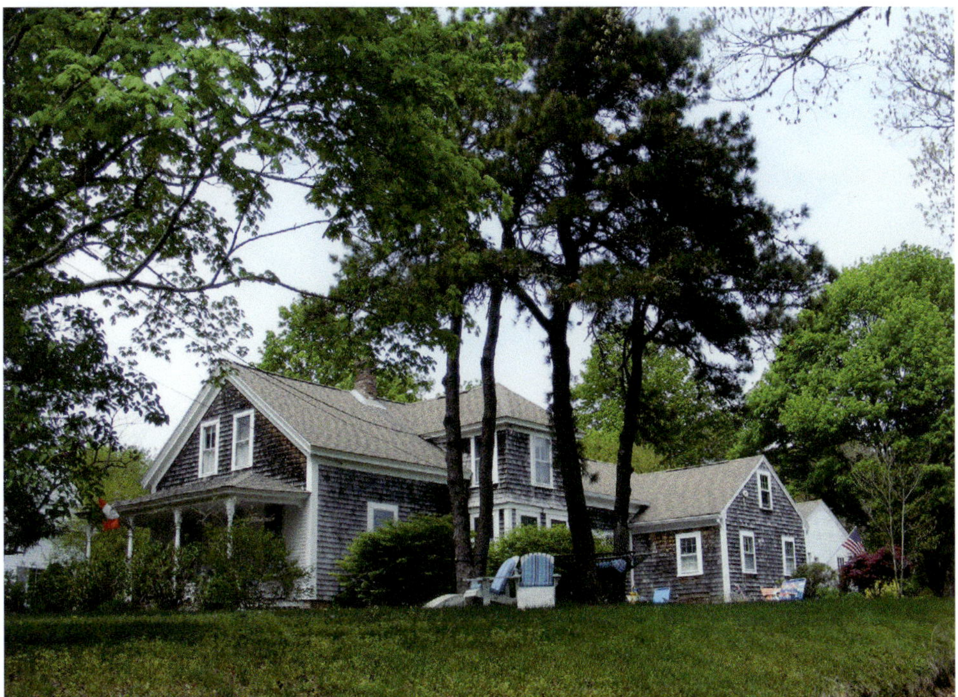

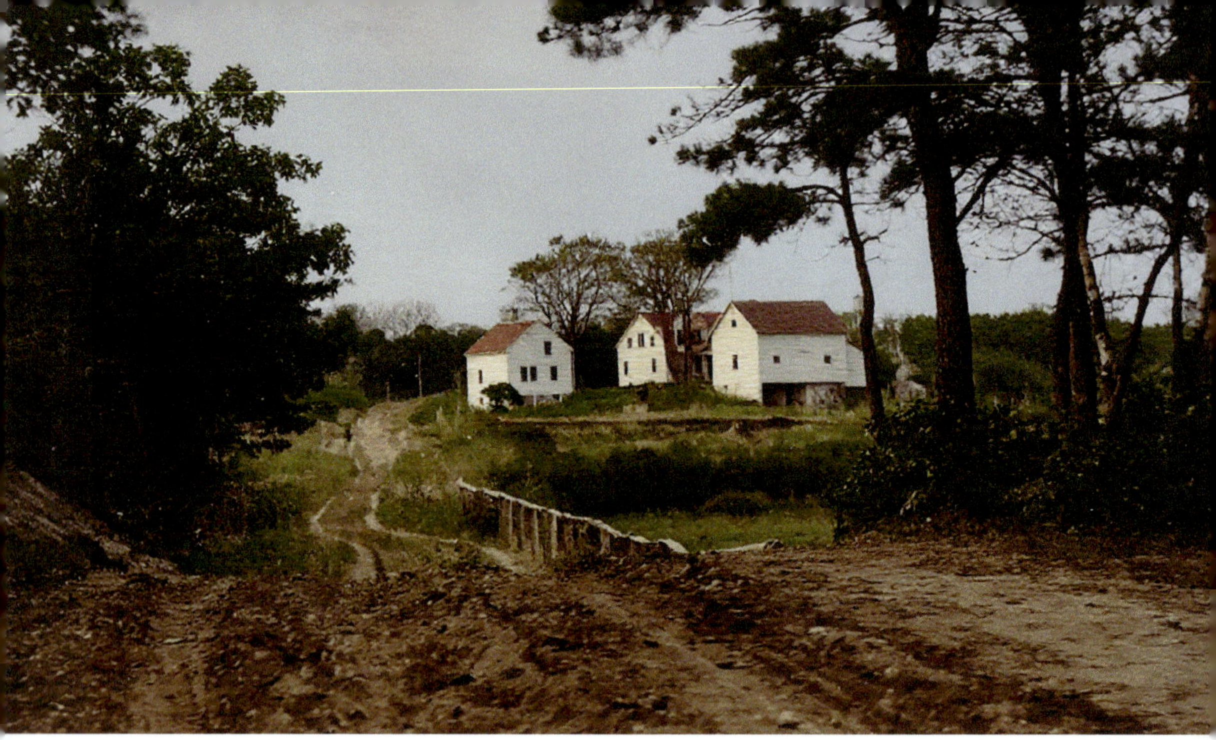

EARLY FARM HOUSES: A pastoral scene of clustered old farmhouses on a dirt road has become the main entrance to a large cluster of well-maintained condominiums. Happily, the farmhouses still stand guard on Forest Street.

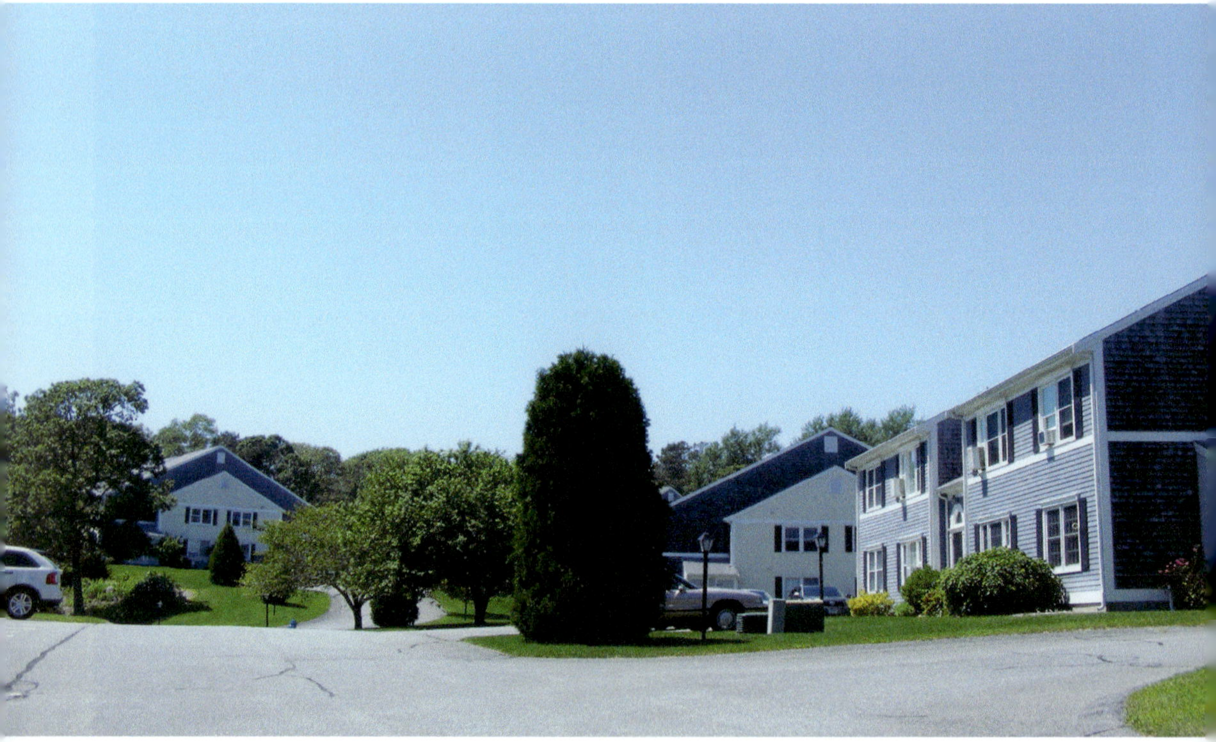

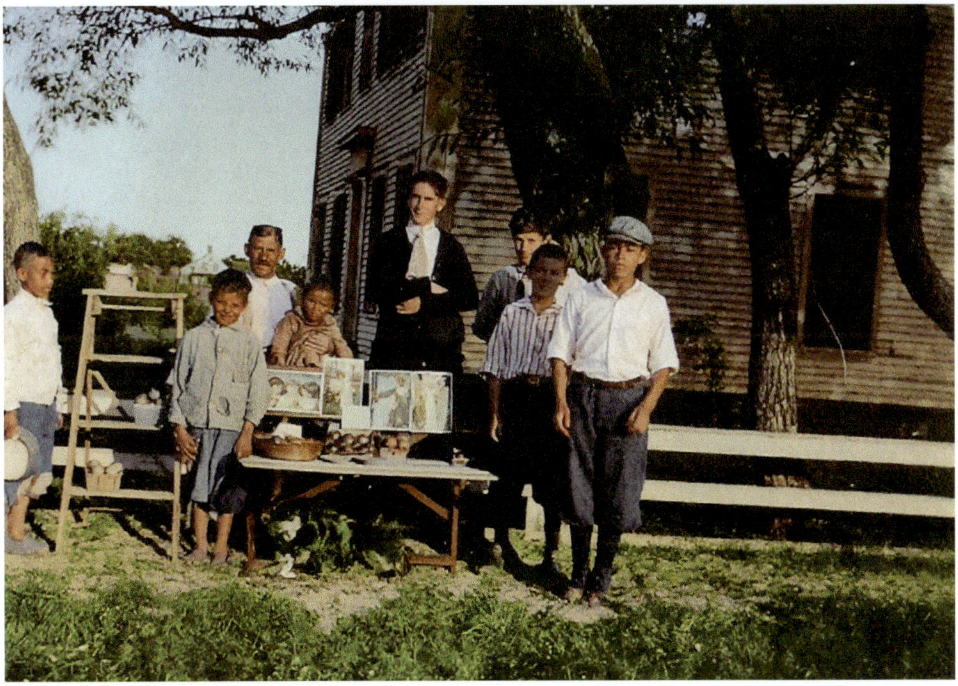

BOYS' APPLE STAND: A bygone road stand provided a means for children to acquire a few coins. Today's marketing of foodstuffs is very different. The popular Farmers' Market meets weekly in season in a park across from Brooks Academy. Shoppers have access to fresh produce, other foodstuffs, and some craft items, while being serenaded by a different musical group each week.

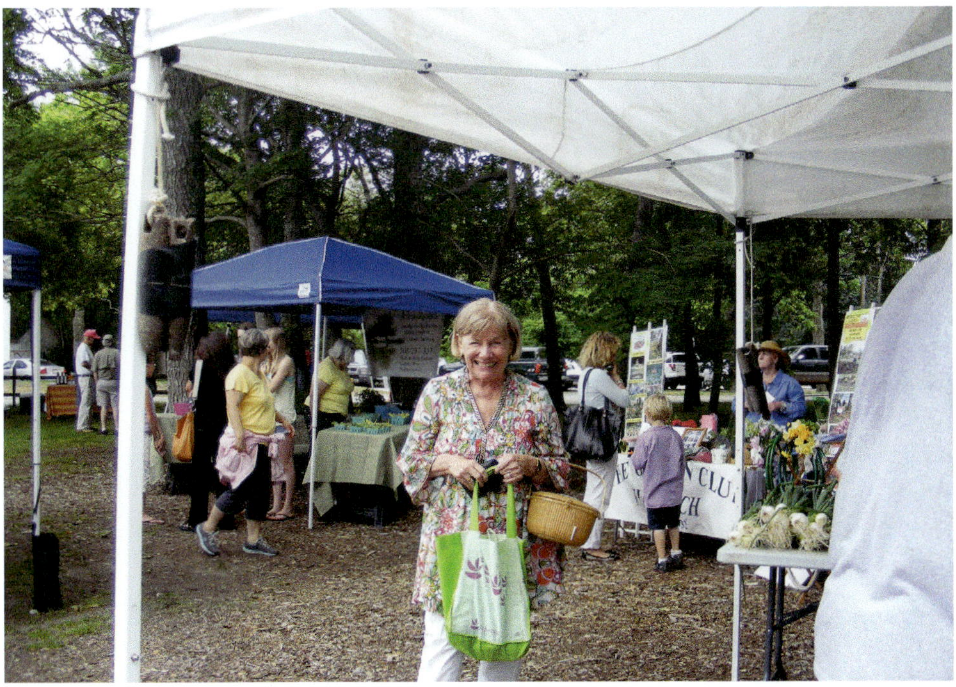

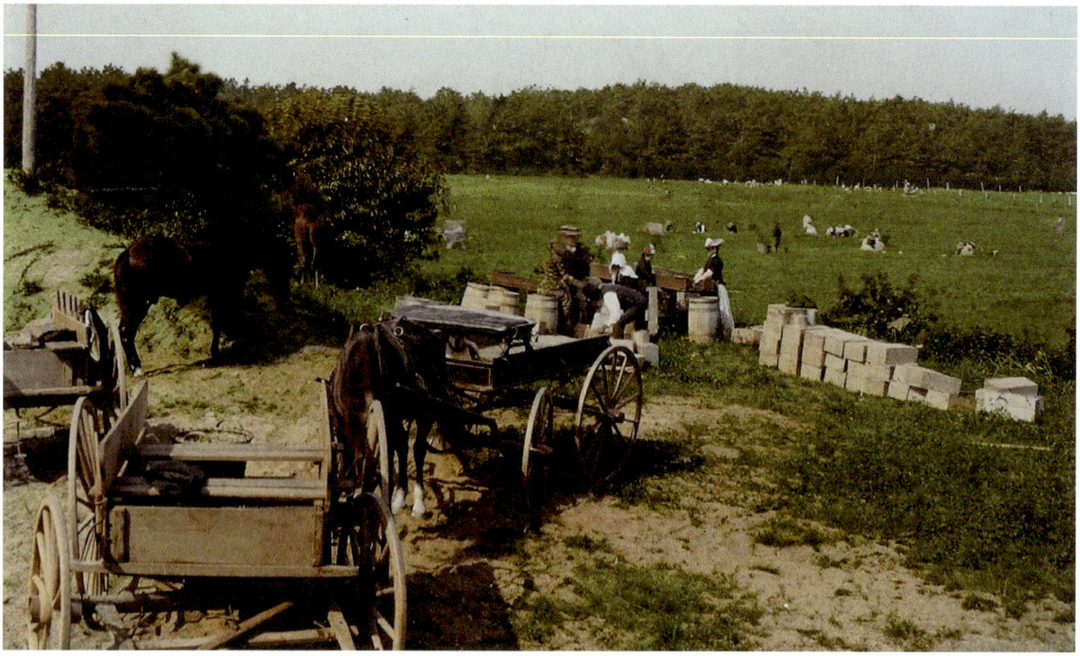

CRANBERRY CULTURE: Utilizing the abundant bog lands and supply of cheap labor, some farmers switched to cultivation of cranberries in the 1840s. The berries were widely sought for their health value and ease of storage. Whole families could earn money helping pick and sort the berries. The income was more than welcome after the economy receded in the 1860s. Now, much of the crop is wet-harvested, using mechanical equipment.

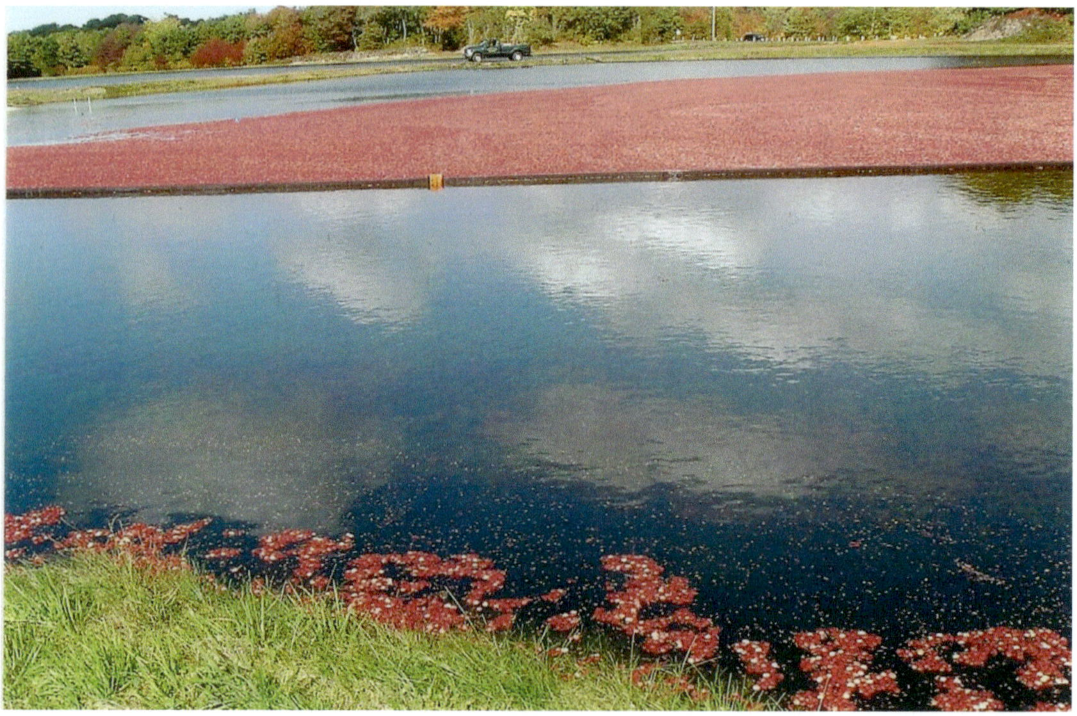

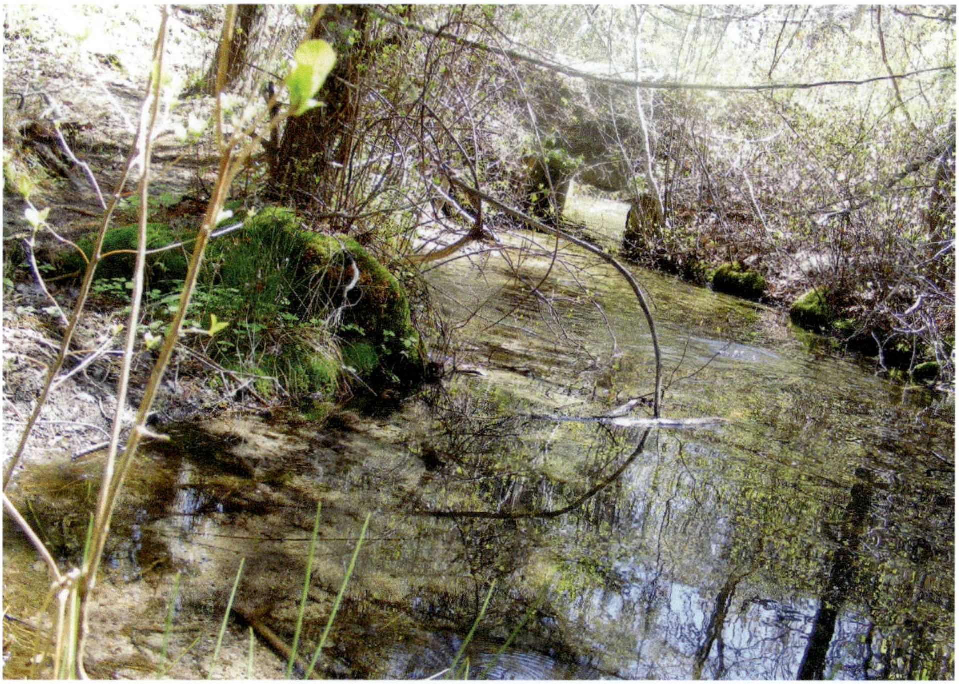

CAHOON'S CANAL: Wet-harvesting requires tapping into pond water. When Alvin Cahoon needed an adequate water supply for his bogs, in 1850, he proceeded to dig a canal 500 feet long and five feet wide between Seymour's Pond (shown in its natural beauty) and his bog. The canal was dug by hand, and took three years to complete.

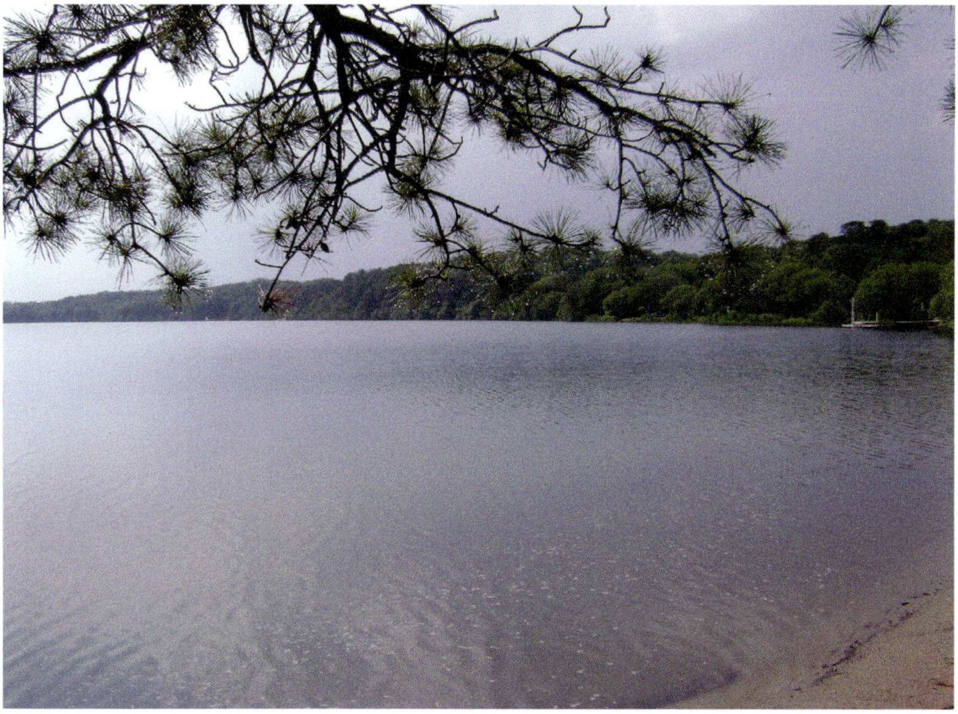

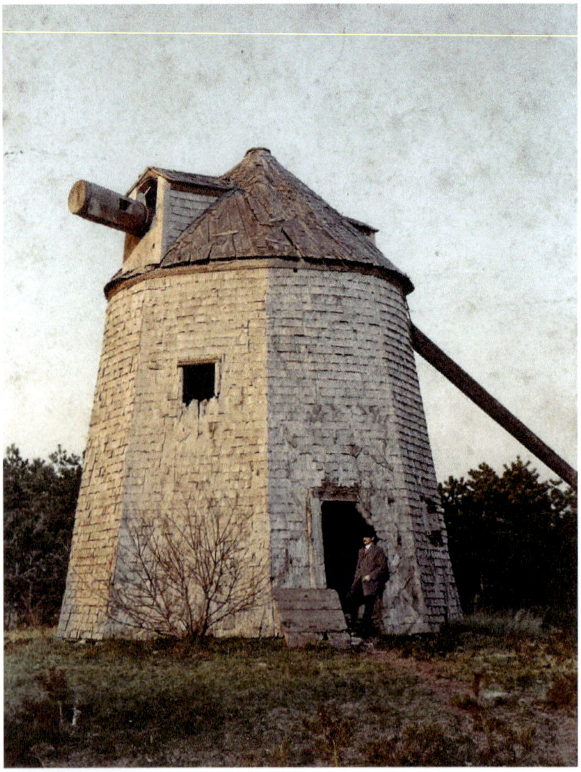

WINDMILL POWER: Wind power was vital to the early community as a means to grind grain. This windmill began operations in Harwich Center and was later moved to Wychmere Harbor. It had fallen into disrepair before 1900. The mill was later rescued and has become an interesting addition to a private home overlooking that harbor.

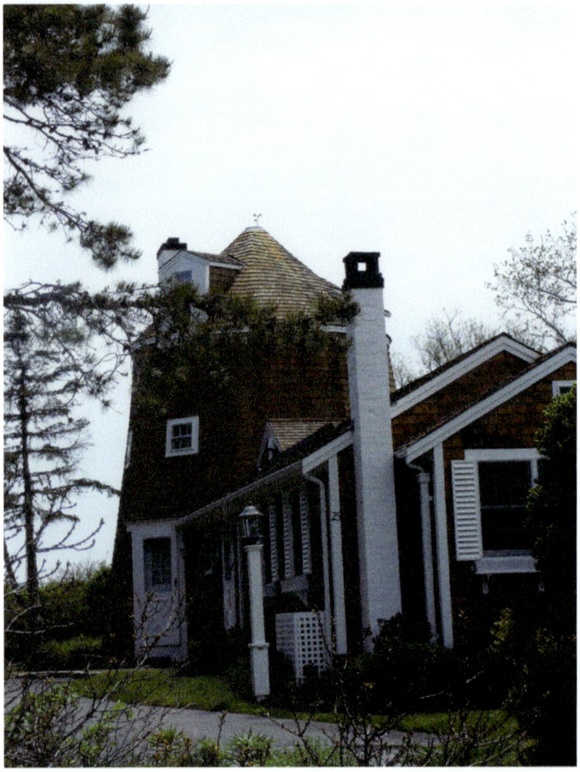

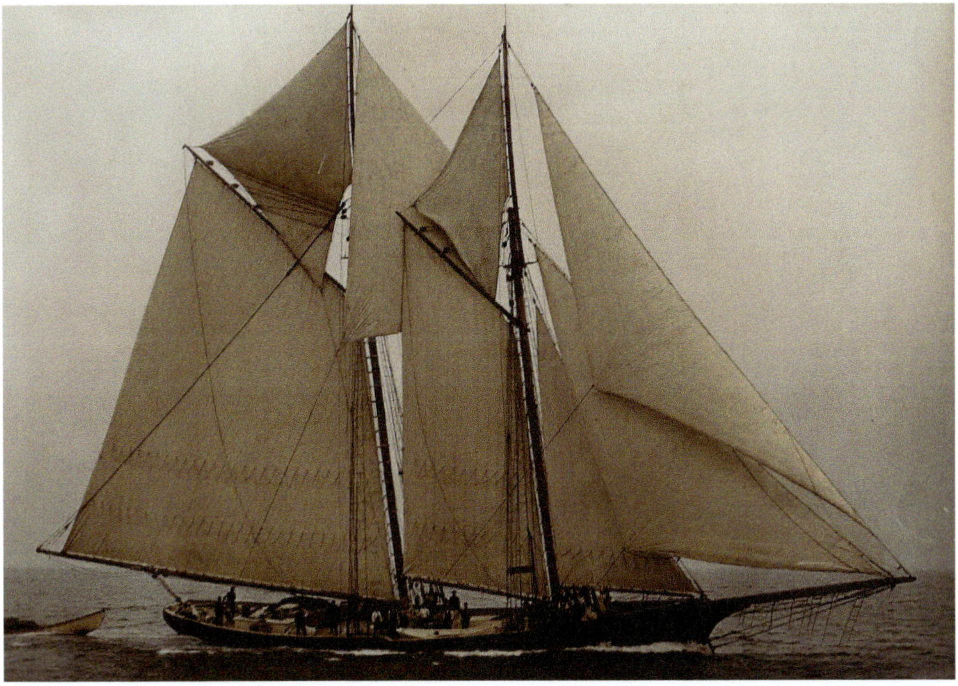

FISHING SCHOONERS: Wind also moved the many ships that sailed from Harwich harbors. The sea supported about two-thirds of the local families, through fishing, carrying cargo on packet boats, or supplying the ships. The two-masted schooner is typical of the boats that fished off George's Banks for cod. The 48-ton yacht built in 1939 continues the town's traditions by providing chartered sails along the beautiful outer Cape coast under the captaincy of Matt Sutphin.

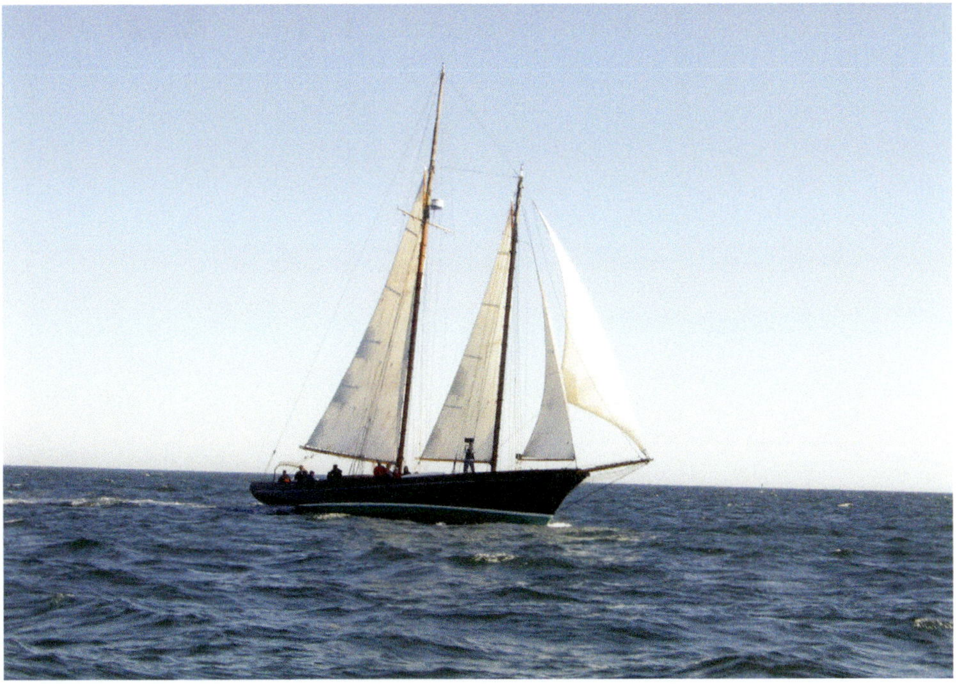

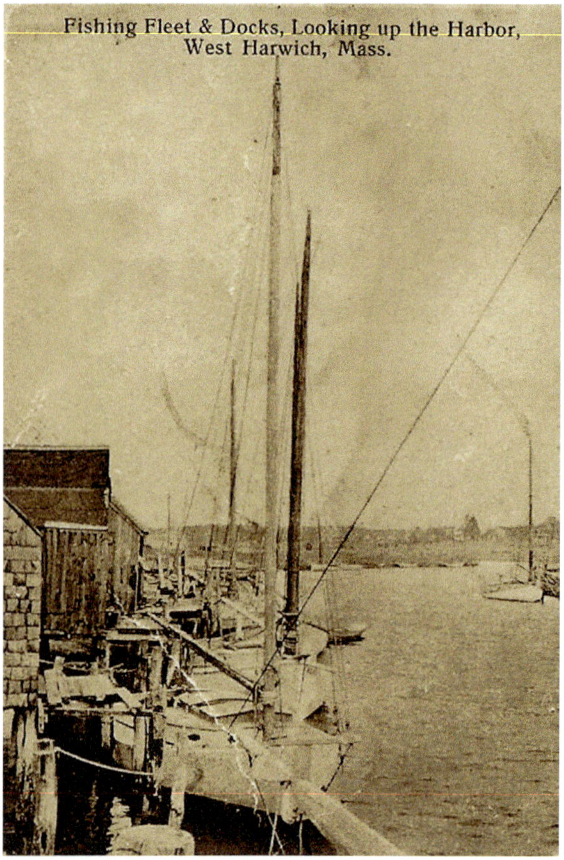

THE HERRING SEINERS: The Herring River, emptying into Nantucket Sound in West Harwich, provided a favored docking area for the fishing fleet. Small boats were better suited to seining the herring. These docks have been replaced by a condominium community.

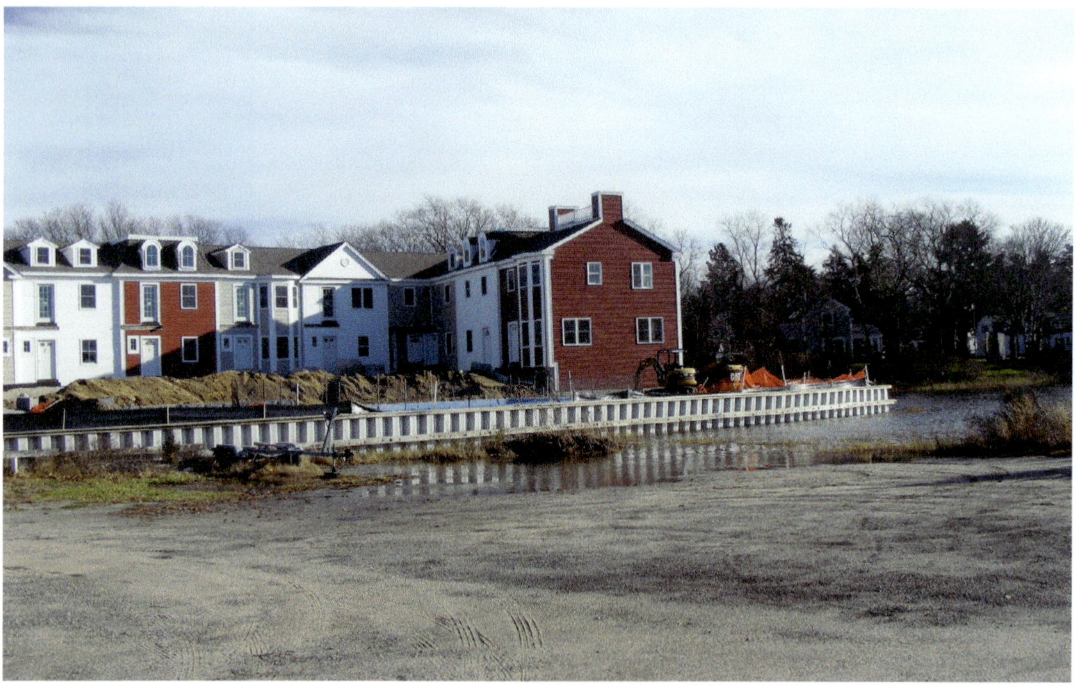

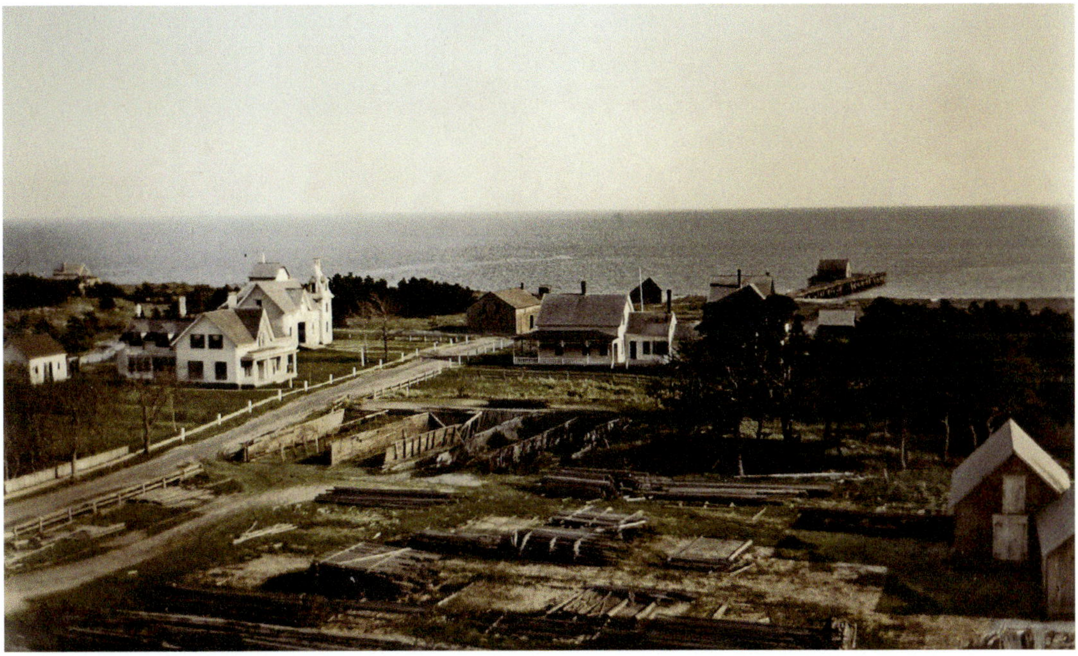

Sea Street Wharf: Lacking a natural deep harbor, piers had to be built out into the Sound to service larger vessels and provide storage and provisions for the ships. This pier at the end of Sea Street enabled the Kelley family to maintain a flourishing coal and lumber business. As ships became larger and often steam-powered, the piers became inadequate and one by one succumbed to coastal storms. The area is now mainly residential.

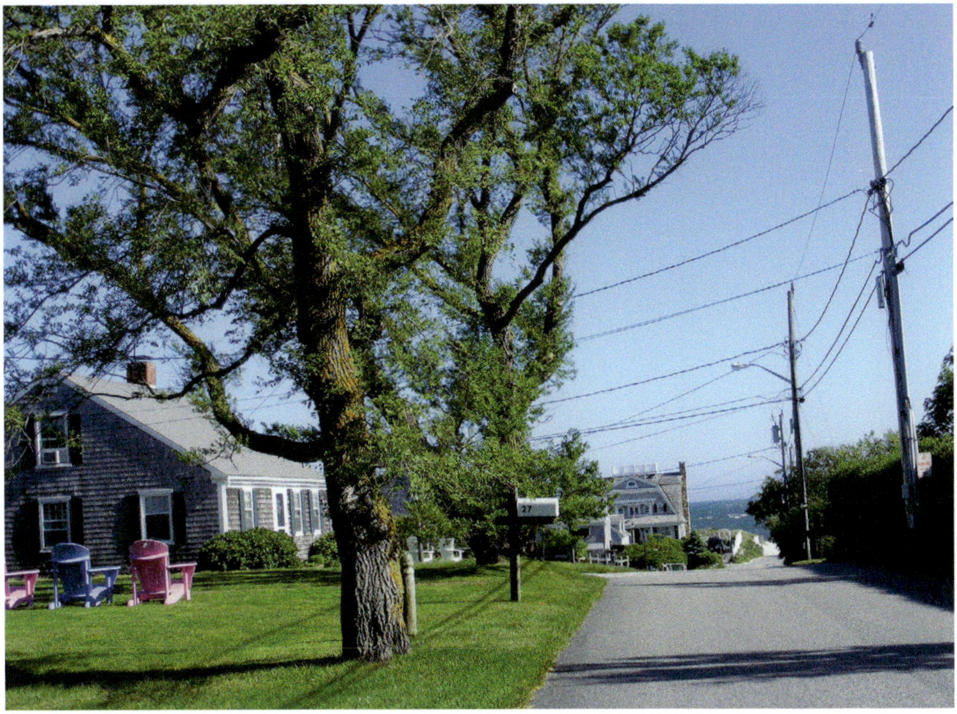

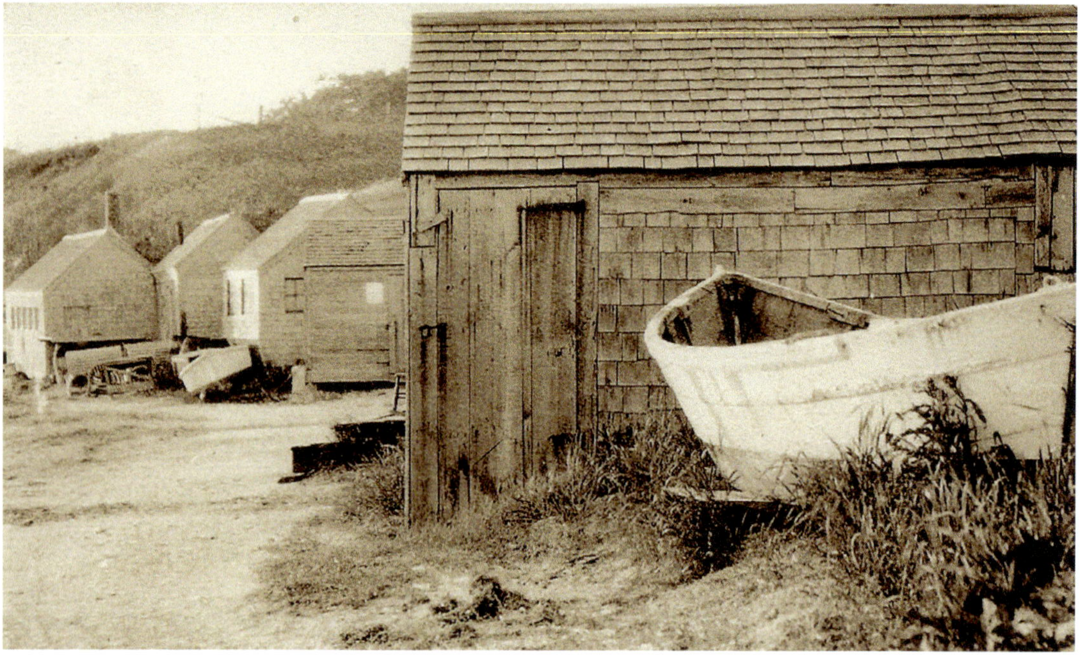

FISHERMEN'S SHACKS: Shanties provided a place to store gear and clean the catch. Several of these shanties at Wychmere Harbor are still used by boat owners who have sometimes modernized them to include electricity.

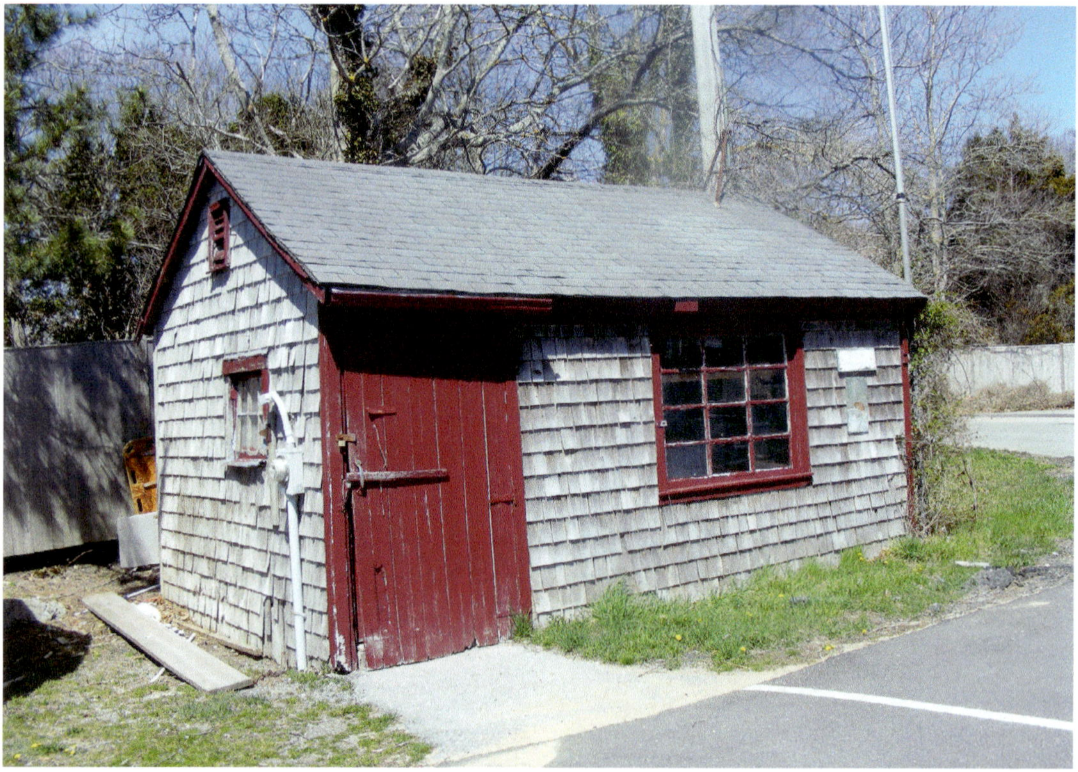

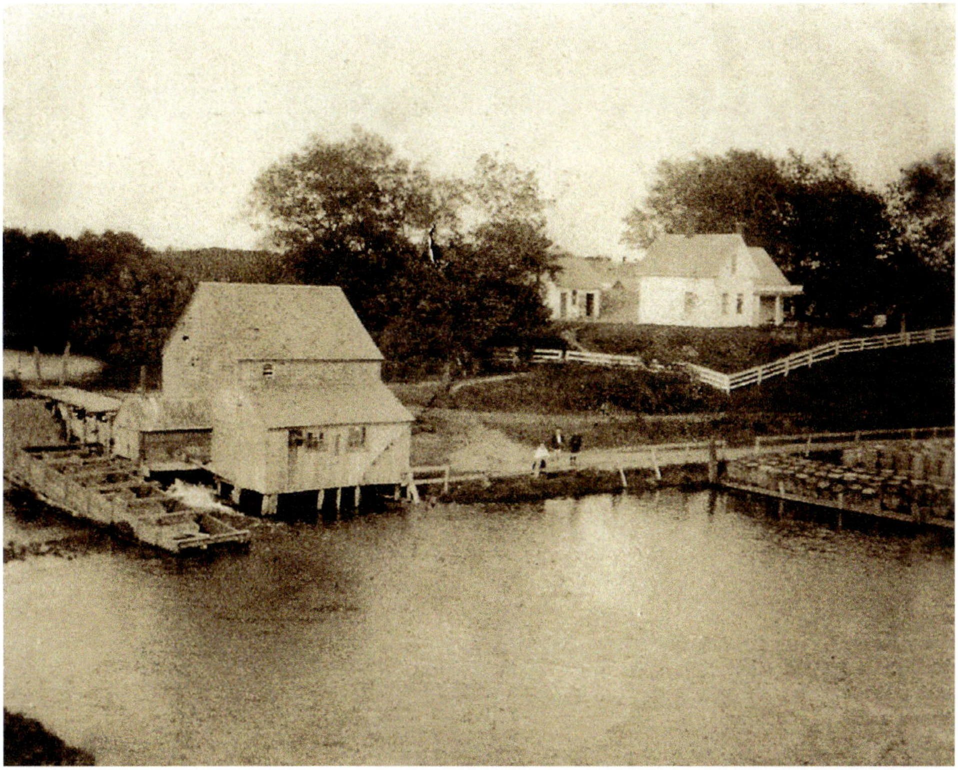

Herring Runs: The annual herring catch was essential to profitable fishing, especially since these smaller fish were the prime local source of bait. Harwich's catch was often among the highest on the Cape. The herring still return each spring, aided by manmade flumes to help them to their spawning areas. Due to past overfishing, however, both state and local regulations now prohibit taking these fish.

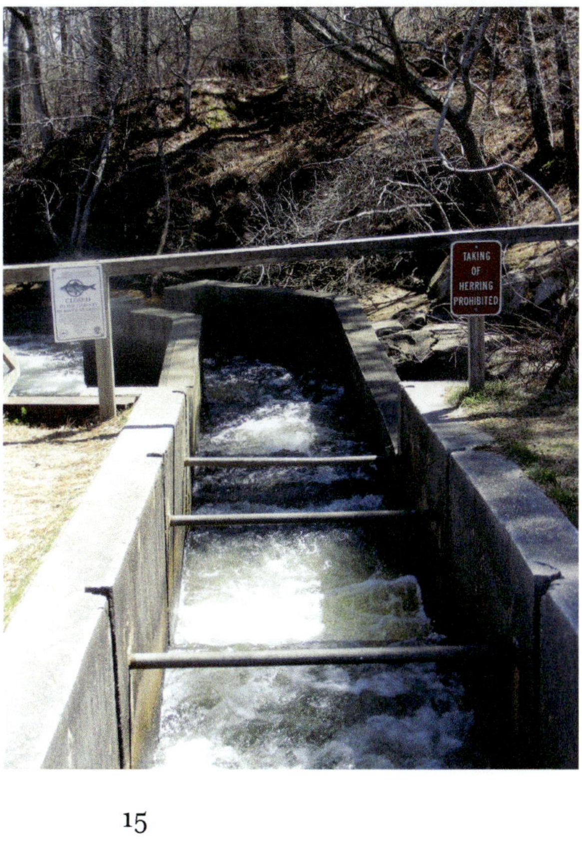

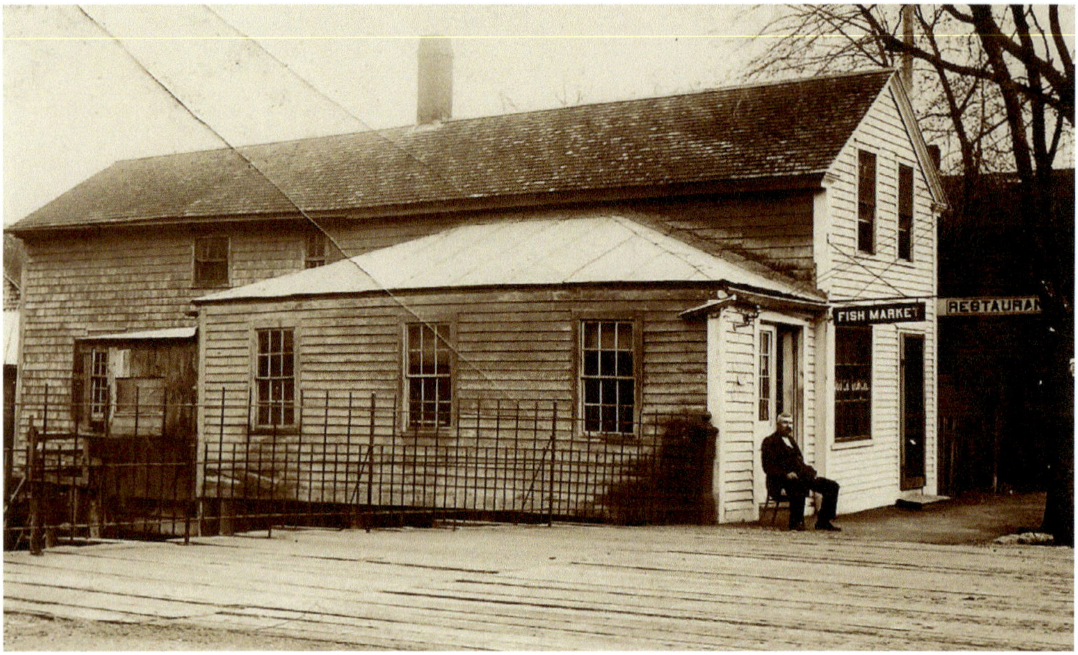

FISH MARKETS: Village fish markets supplied area residents. Alton Robbins maintained this one at the busy corner of Bank and Main Streets in Harwich Port. It is now the outlet for Kreeger Pottery and a charming residence.

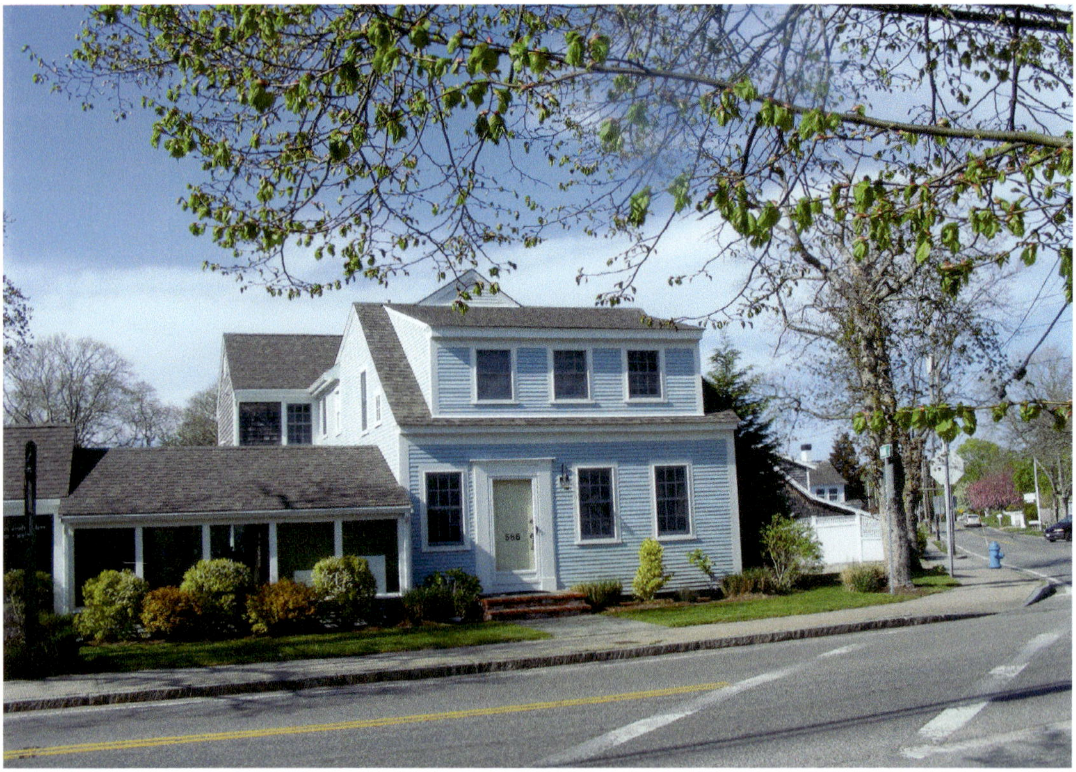

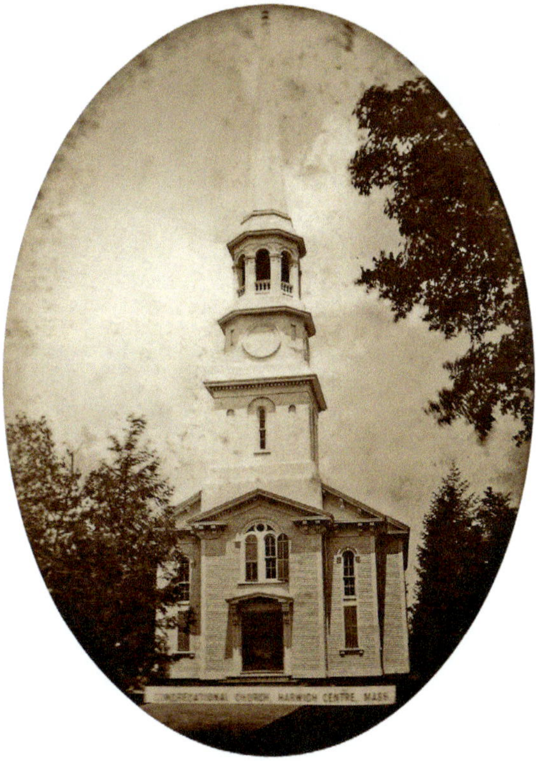

First Congregational Church:

In 1694, Harwich colonists were granted the right to organize a town although boundaries were not set until the 1803 separation from Brewster. For several more decades residents were required by law to support the established church. In 1747, Harwich worshippers had been allowed to form their own meeting house in the Center to avoid the journey to Brewster for services. This First Congregational Church has continued to physically and intellectually occupy a central role in the community. The present church, often photographed, has retained its character since its dedication in 1855.

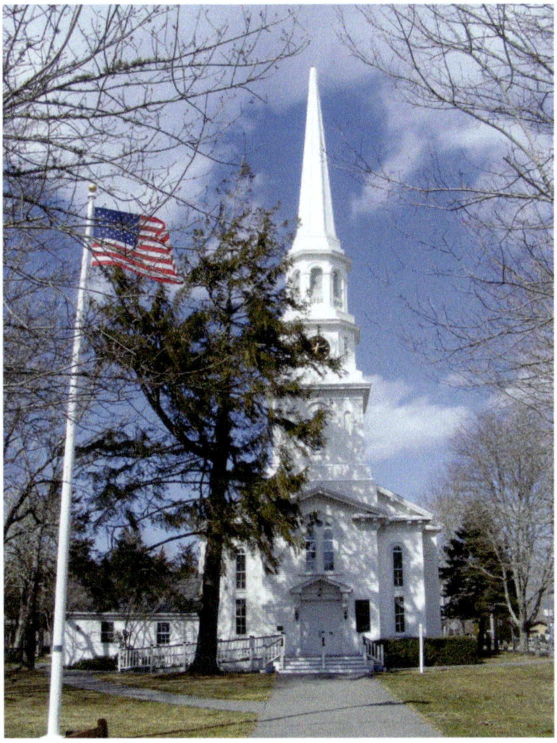

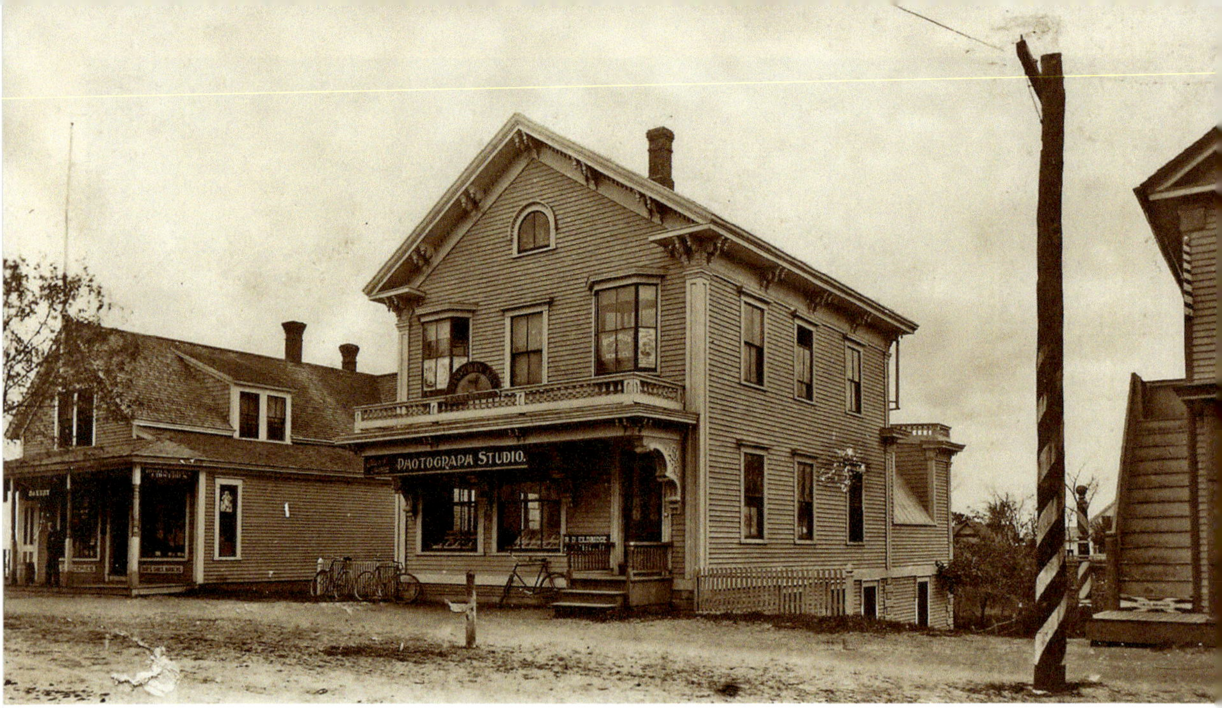

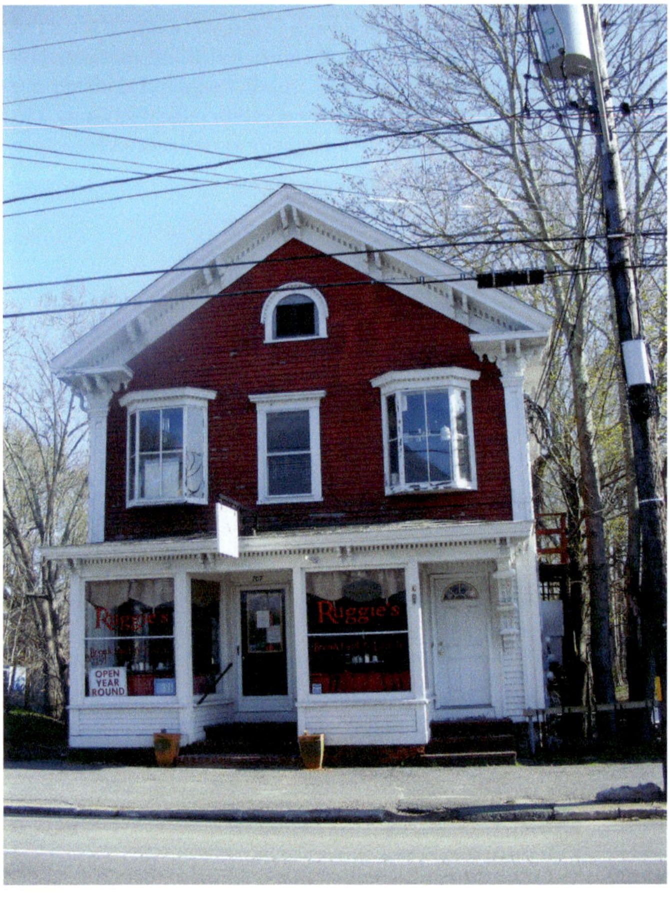

MAIN STREET SHOPPING: Clement A. Cahoon's photographic studio in this Main Street general store was particularly profitable during the Civil War. Families craved images of those men going to war. The building is little changed and is a popular small café.

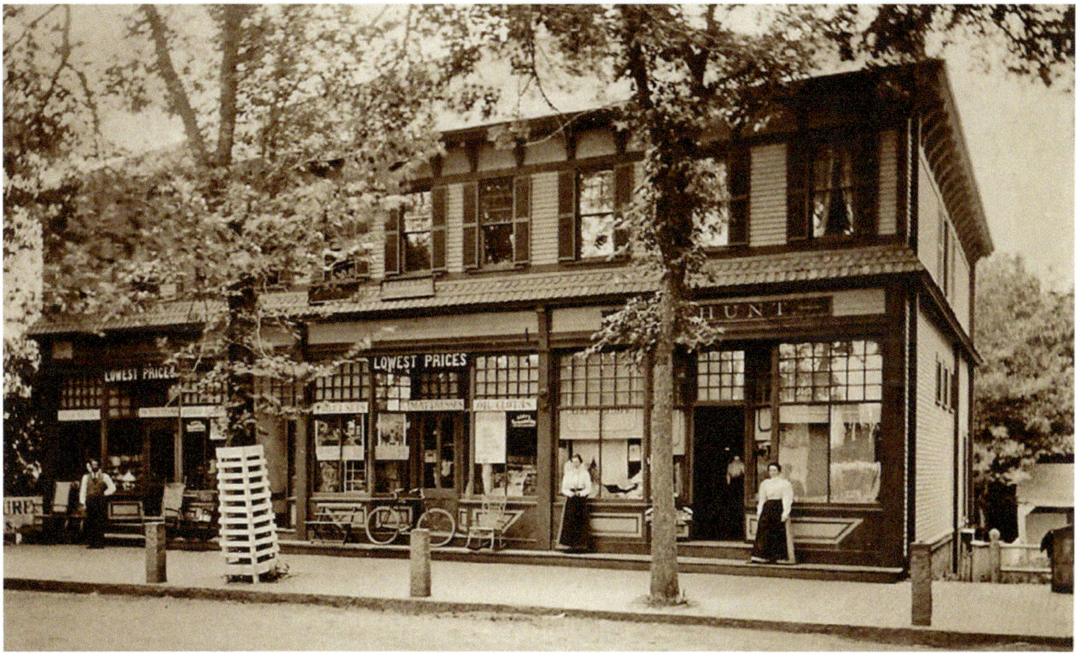

BROOKS BLOCK: Henry Brooks had become a wealthy Boston merchant when he built this multipurpose structure in the 1880s next to the house where he had been born. Rental from the ground level shops provided the means to reserve the second floor for the Pilgrim Masonic Lodge, veterans of the Civil War, and space for the town's first free library. The Brooks Library now occupies all of this enlarged facility: it is one of the busiest libraries on the Cape.

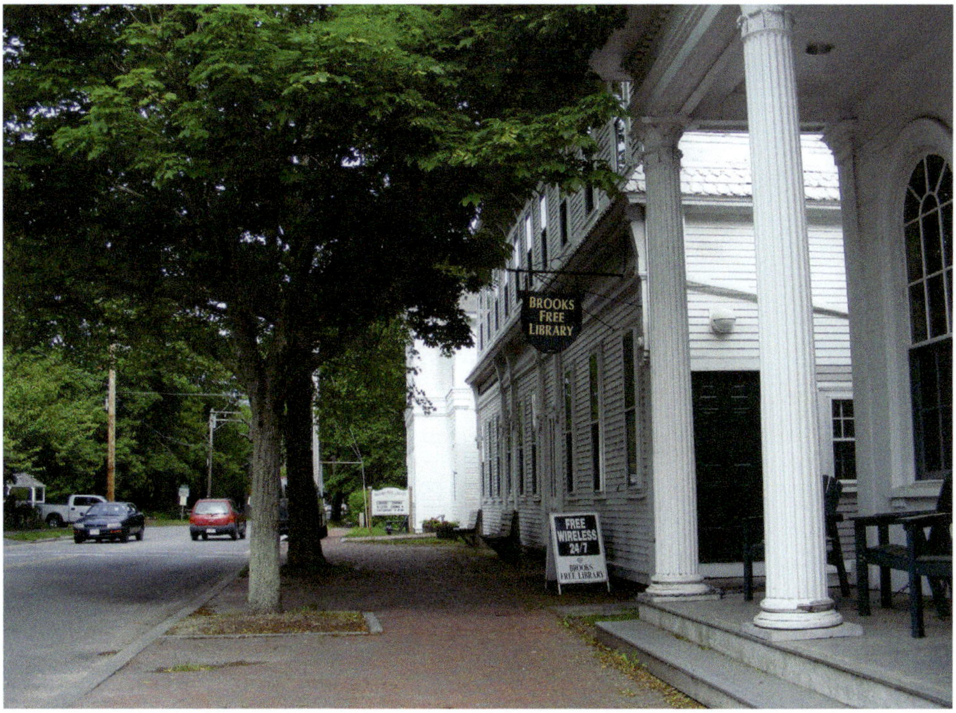

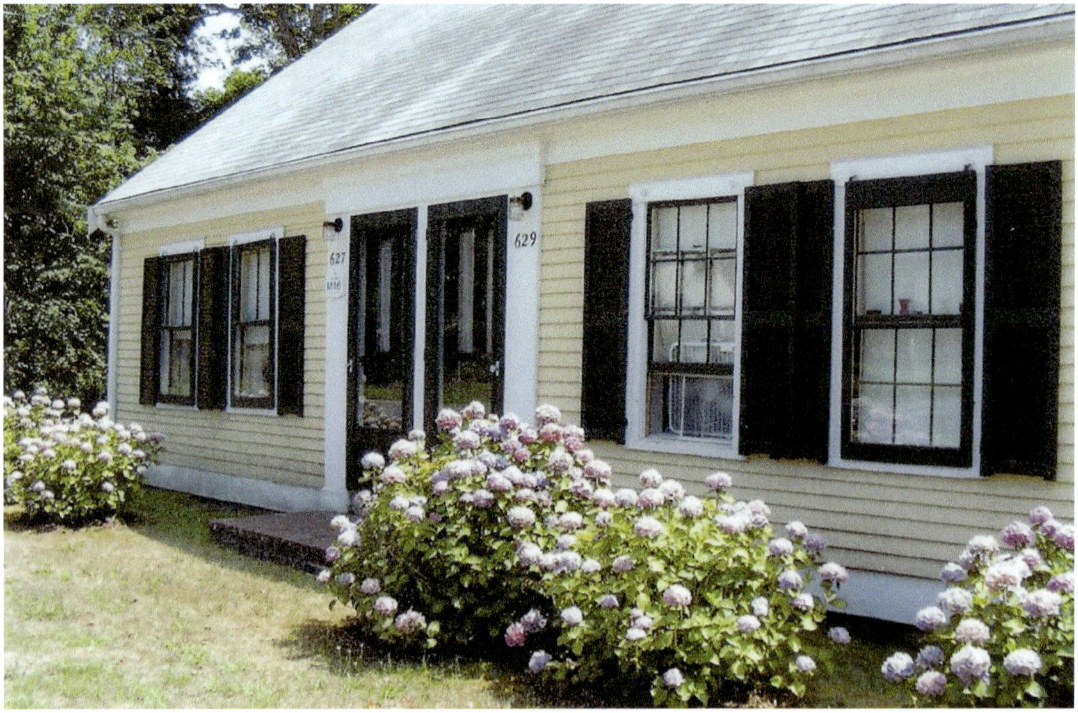

DOUBLE HOUSES: Duplexes new? This double house was moved from North Harwich to Harwich Center in 1816. The Baker and Hendren families had completely independent living areas. In 1967, new owners combined the two interiors, retaining the old wooden pegged beams and other woodwork. They proudly retained the two exterior house numbers to honor the past.

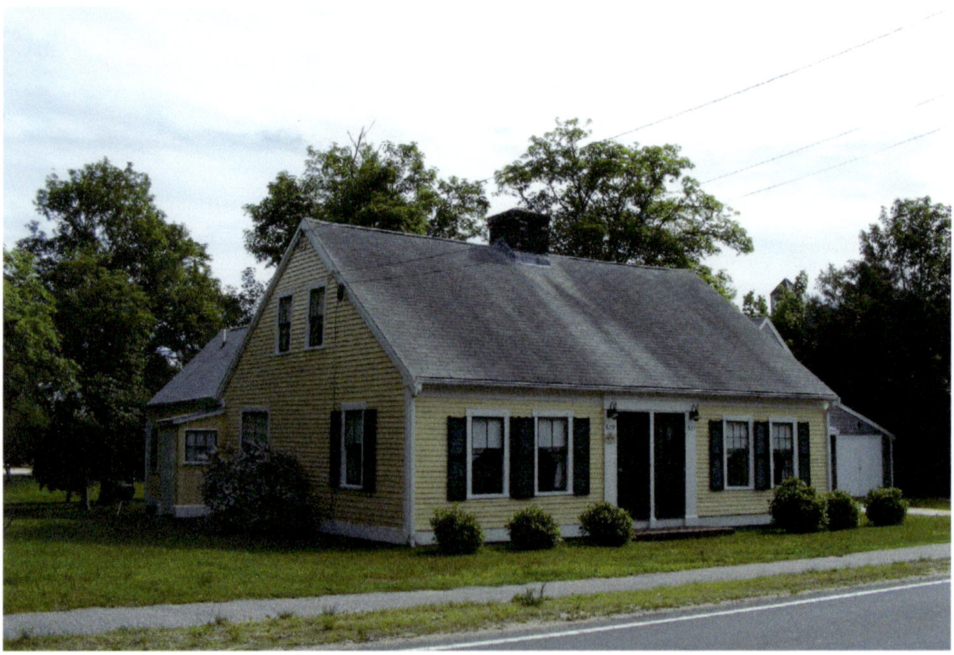

CHESTER SNOW'S ESTATE: An inventor and investor, Chester Snow meant his home to be a village show-piece. He built and operated the Exchange Building. He was also largely responsible for bringing the telegraph and the railroad to Harwich, and even building a racetrack in Harwich because of his love of horses. After his death the plan to make his home into an area hospital failed. The house was razed after being badly damaged by a hurricane. The site now holds an apartment complex.

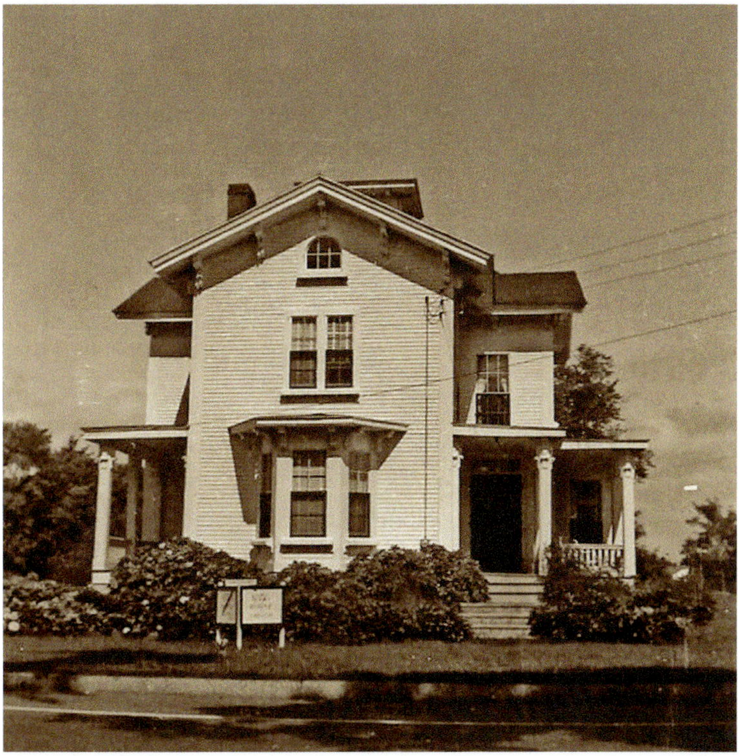

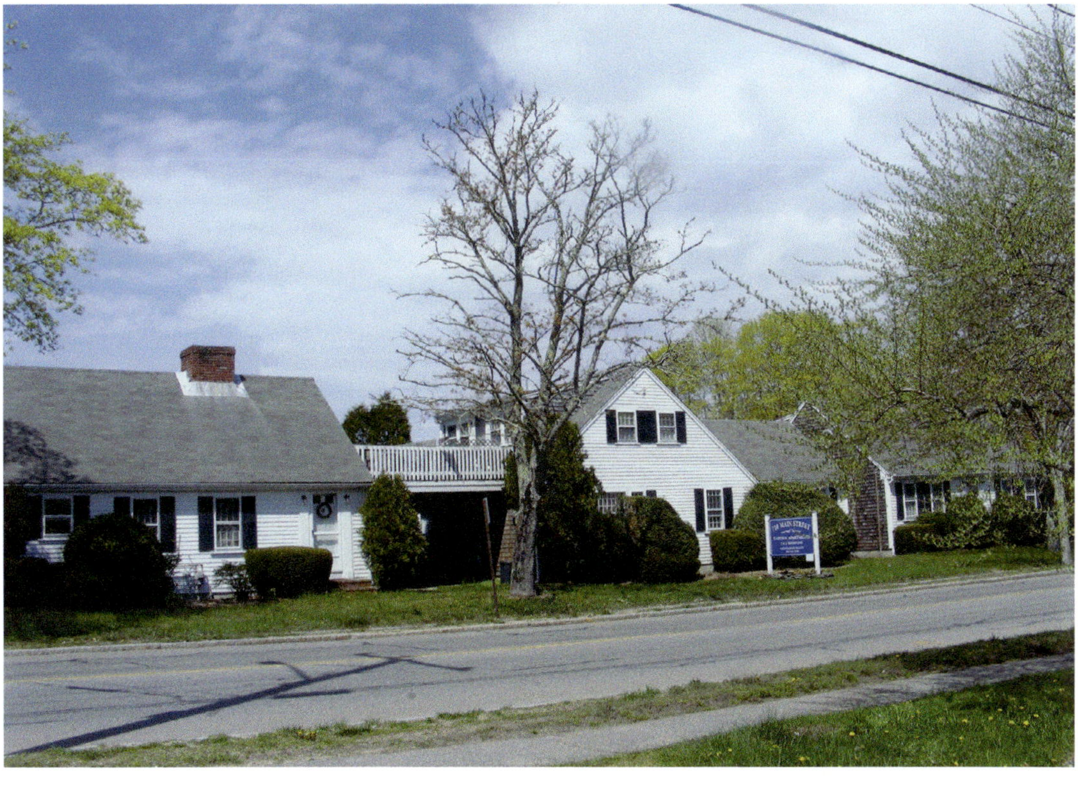

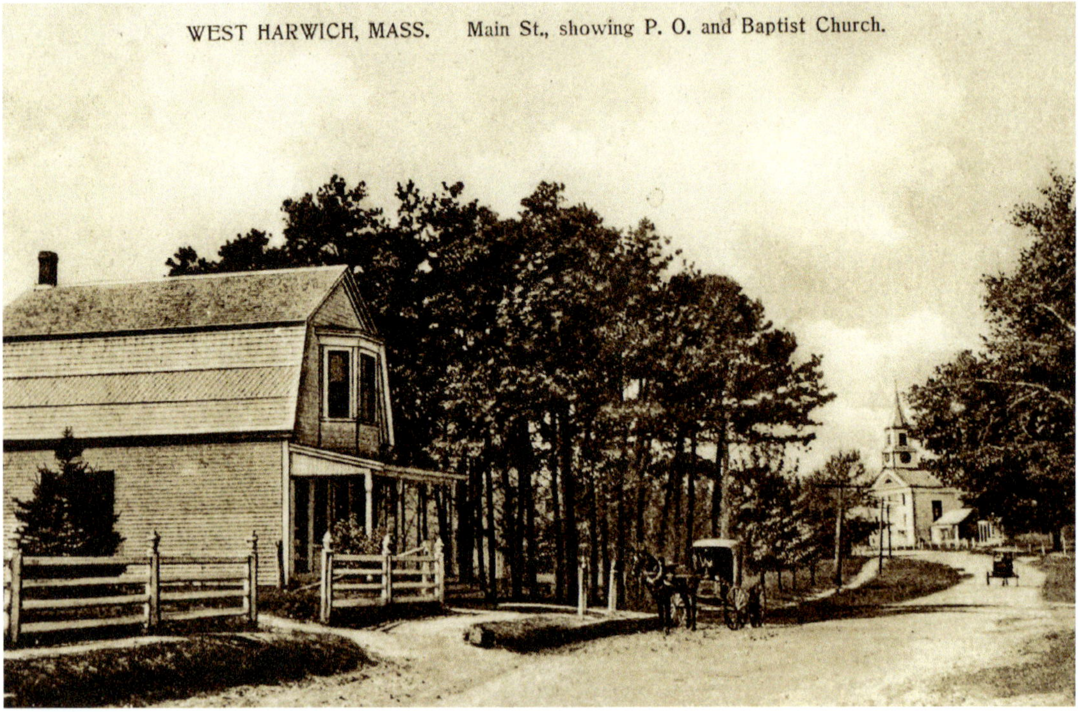

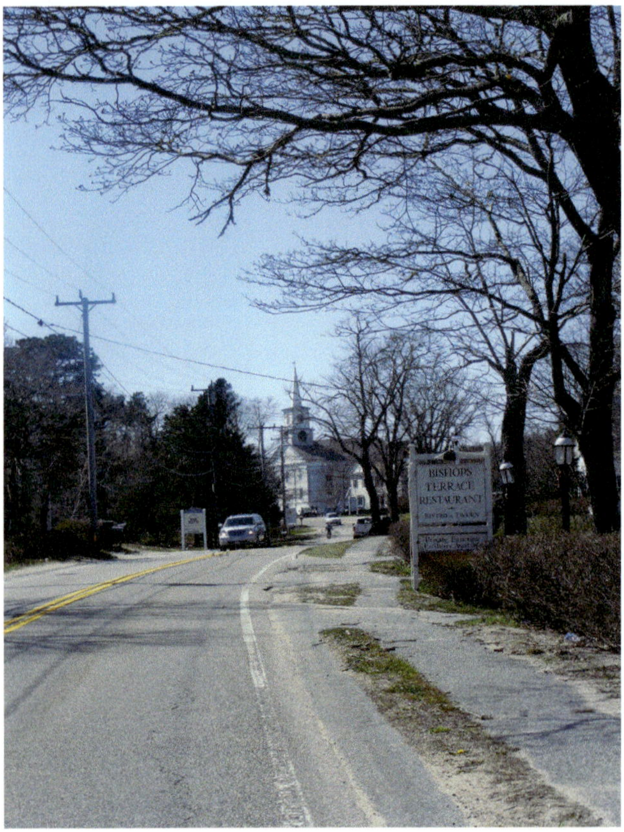

WEST END OF HARWICH:
The bend in the road near the Dennisport line provides dramatic focus in this early photograph, replicated in a contemporary one. Many sea captains chose to build their homes in this village, both because of the proximity to the Herring River and the attractiveness of the neighborhood.

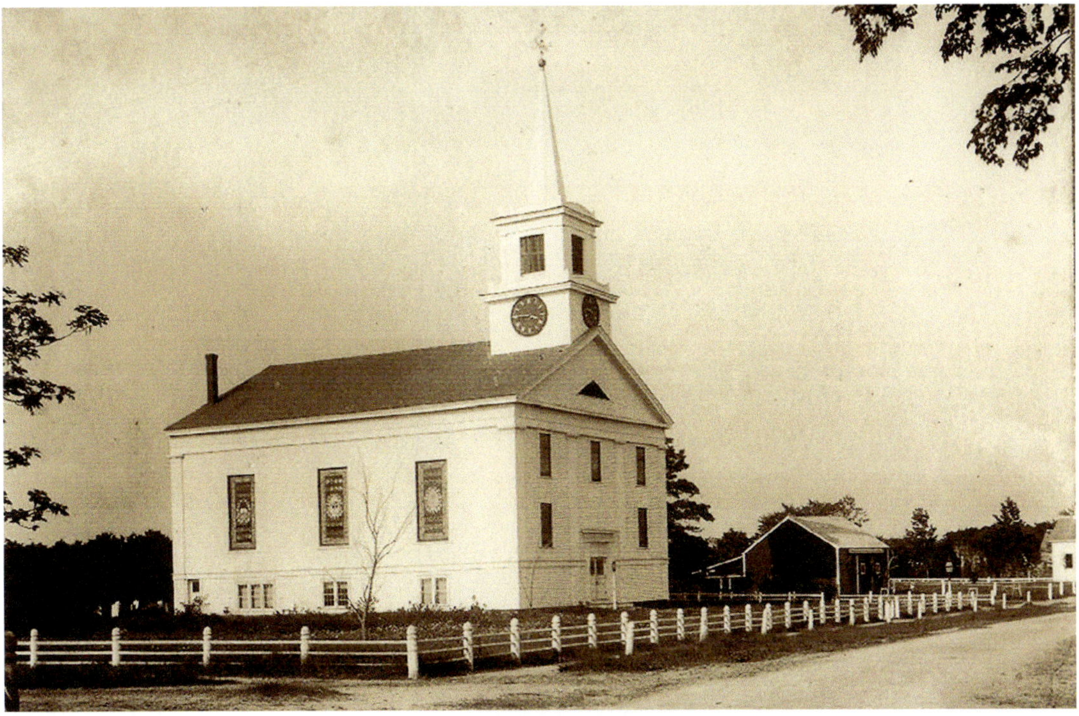

West Harwich Baptist Church: Organized in 1828 by Baptists from North Harwich, this impressive building is the oldest Baptist Church on Cape Cod. The church was rebuilt in 1841 in Greek Revival style. Its stained glass windows were a gift from Caleb Chase a half century later. The church steeple still dominates the area. And the original clock still tells the time.

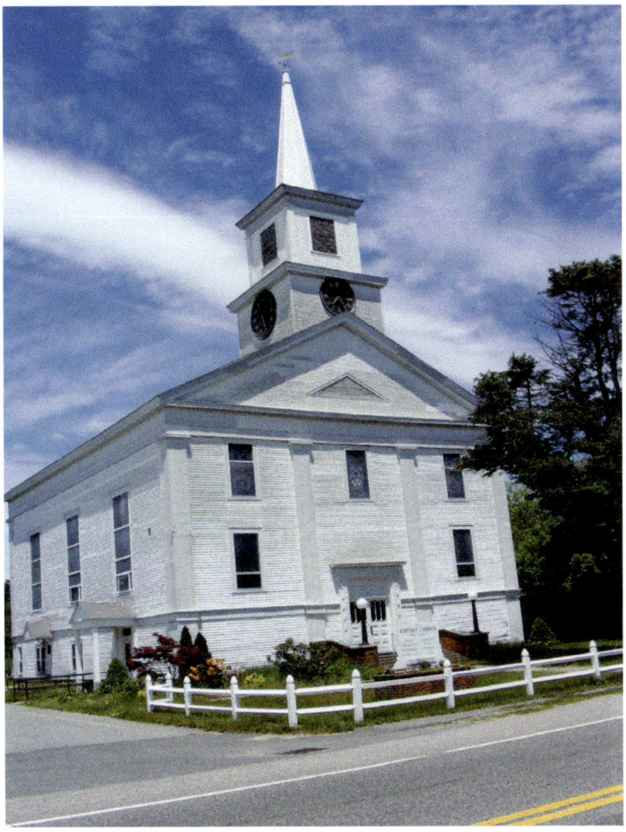

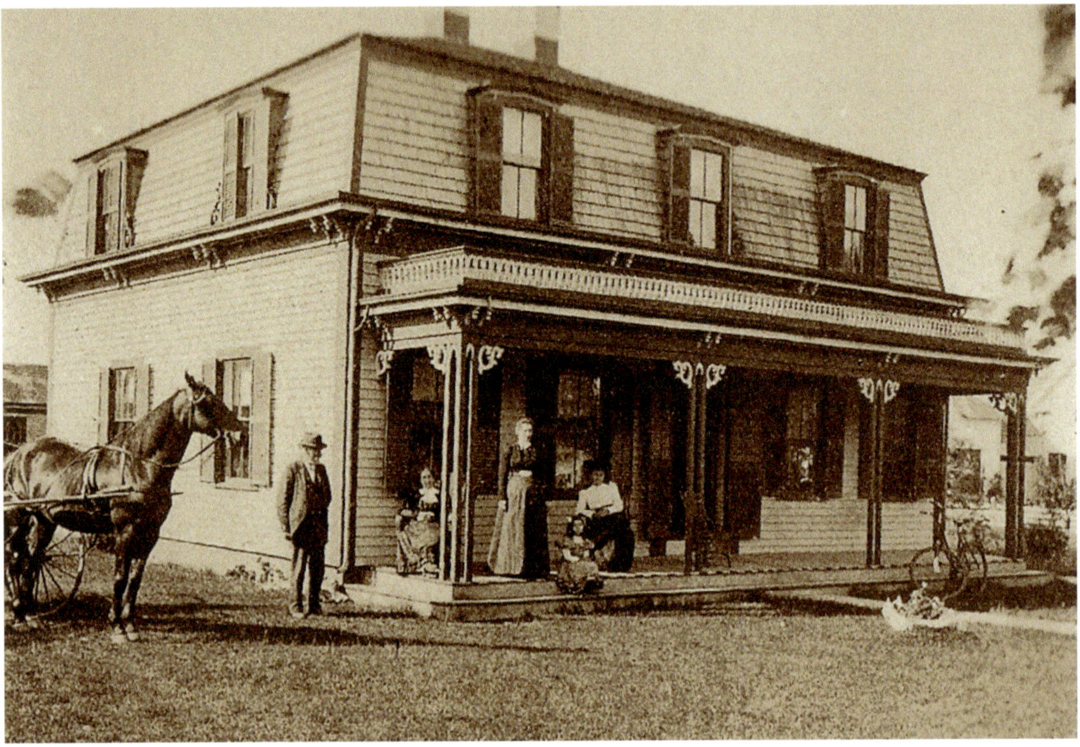

OLDE HARWICH LODGING: Welcoming the weary traveler, this lodge was originally built as a home for a sea captain, Jeremiah Parke. In about 1960, an addition was joined to the home and the premises were converted to today's Olde Harwich Lodgings. This motor inn has carefully retained many of the quaint features of the old homestead.

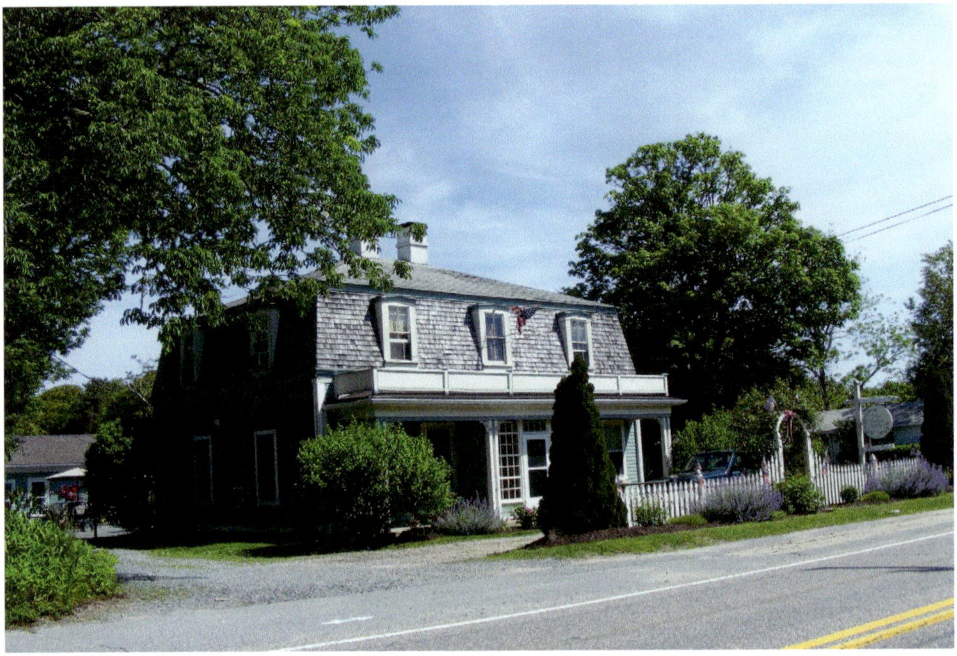

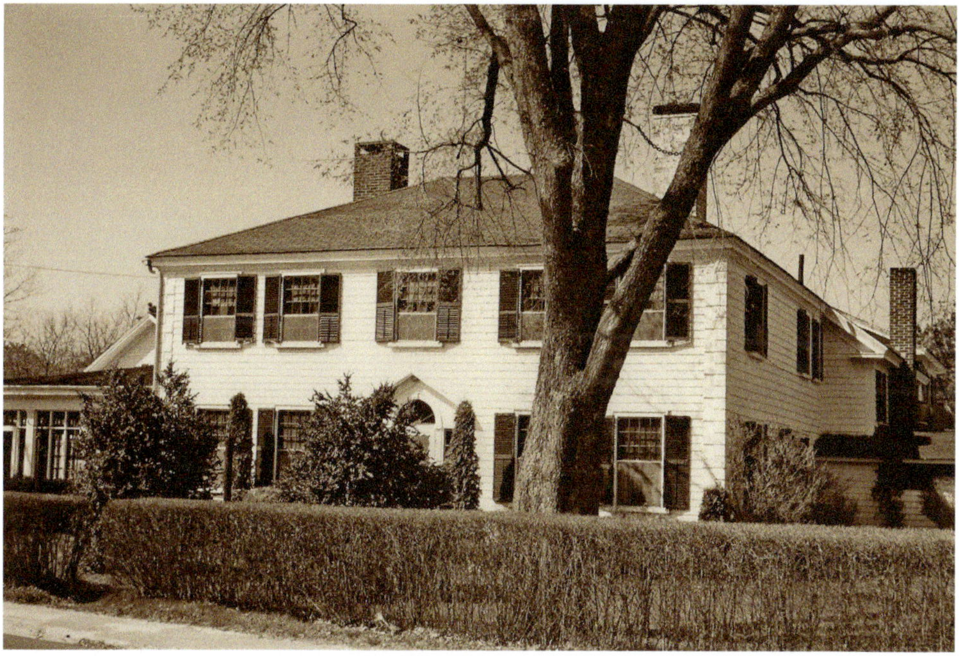

JOB CHASE'S ESTATES: Job Chase and his many descendants (he had seventeen children) were long prominent in West Harwich. Born in 1736, Job acquired vast land holdings around the Herring River, and made a fortune with his fishing fleets. Among the houses he built for his family is this Georgian style home. After the Second World War, the property was purchased by the Bishop family, and wings were added to provide for the very popular Bishops Terrace Restaurant.

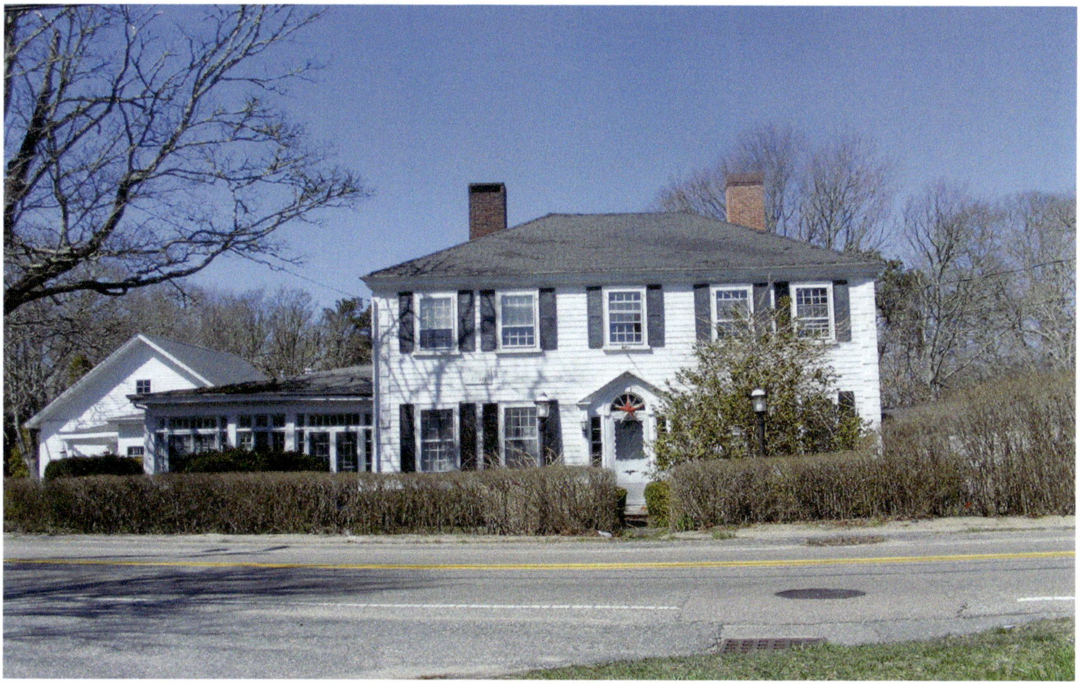

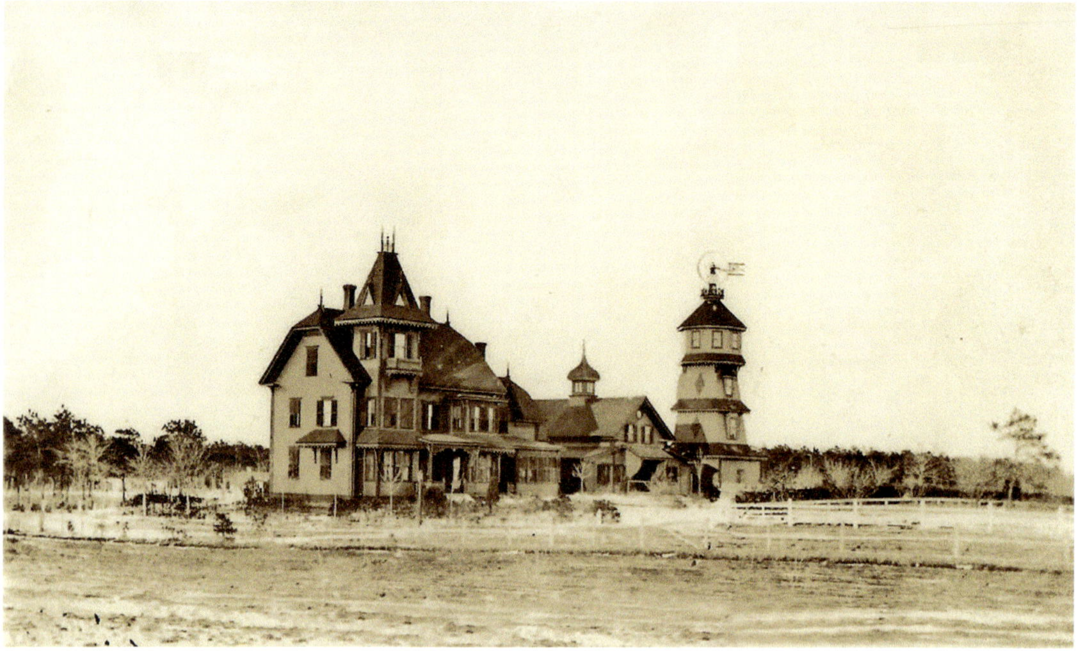

GINGERBREAD HOUSE: After serving in both the Army and Navy during the Civil War, David Ginn earned his medical degree from Harvard and opened his practice in Dennisport. He built this grand mansion on the Harwich side, however, after he married into the Chase family. Ginn was an honored physician, and also became a prominent businessman in West Harwich and in the Port. Dr. Ginn's estate today is the Gingerbread House.

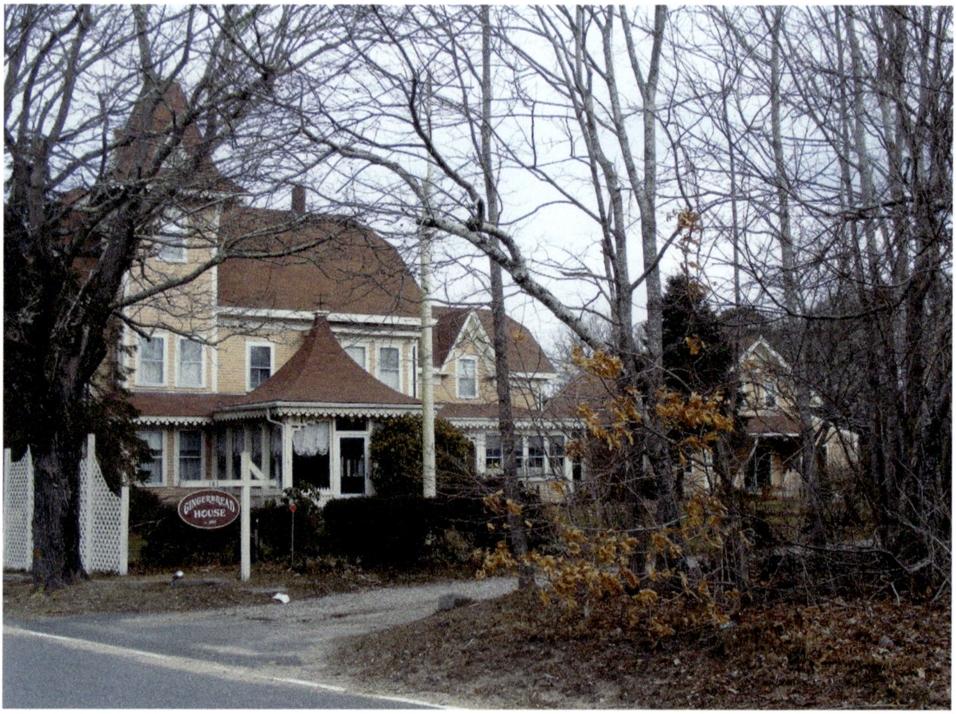

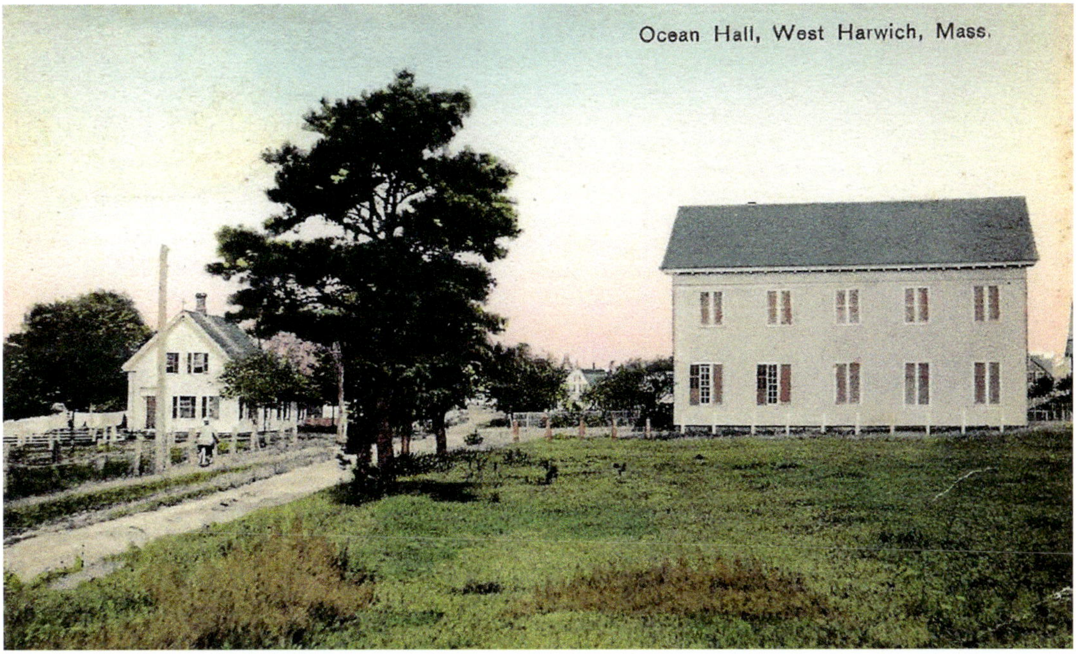

THE JUNIOR THEATRE: When built in 1865 at a cost of $7,000, Ocean Hall was the largest structure in West Harwich. The ground floor was a public hall and the second was used by the Mt. Horeb Lodge of Free Masons. In more recent years, the building has become the main stage for the outstanding productions of the Harwich Junior Theatre.

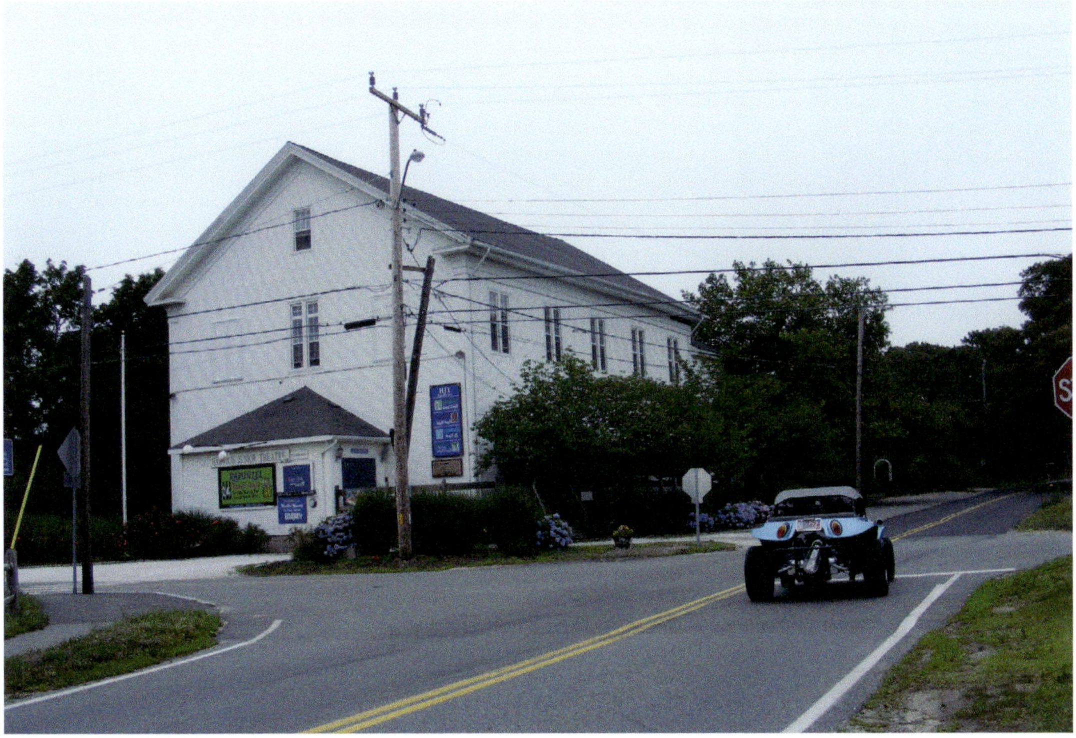

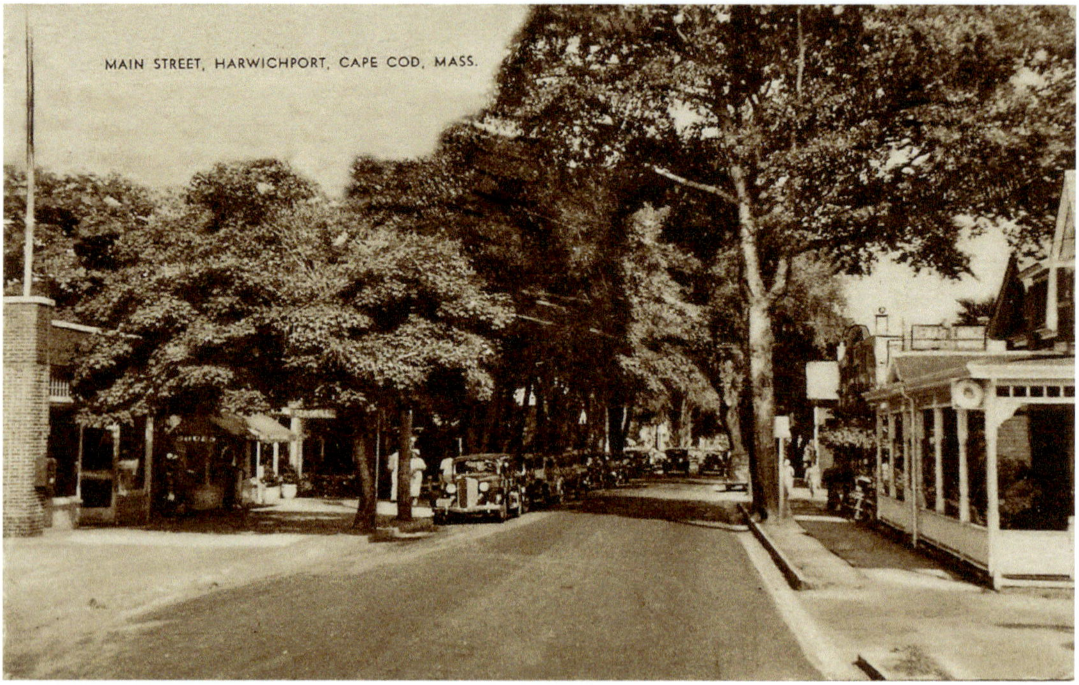

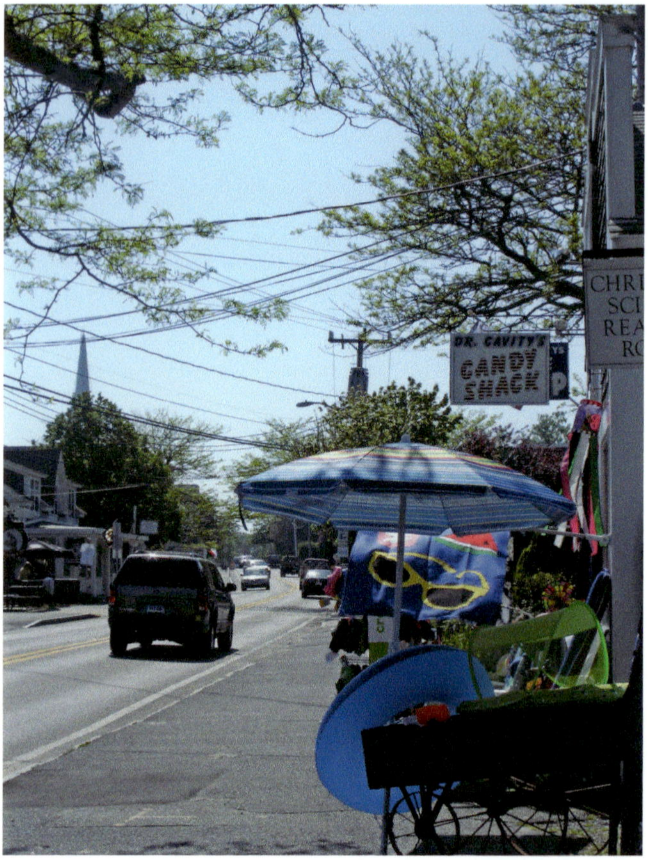

Harwich Port Shops:

Visitors to the Port are greeted by charming scenes such as these along Main Street. The Port provides many small specialty shops and restaurants: very enjoyable musical strolls entertain the shoppers in the summer evenings and before Christmas.

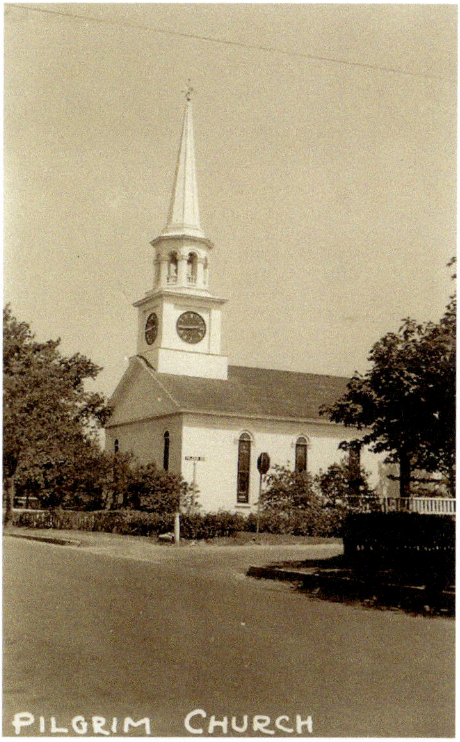

PILGRIM CONGREGATIONAL CHURCH: A much beloved focal point in Harwich Port, the church's steeple is still used as a beacon by mariners in Nantucket Sound. The Congregation was established in 1854 by nearby residents, who claimed they were exhausted by the long trek to Harwich Center to attend services. The church steeple still provides a beacon for water craft in Nantucket Sound. The beauty of the church is retained by careful on-going restoration.

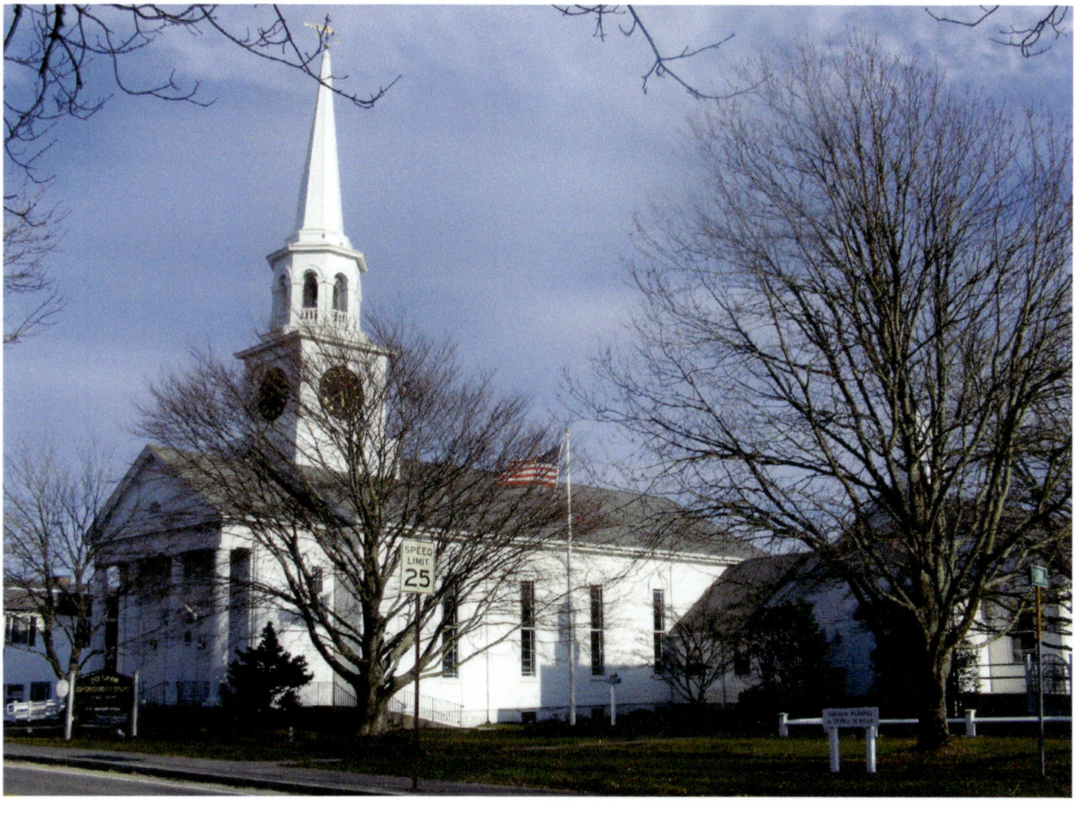

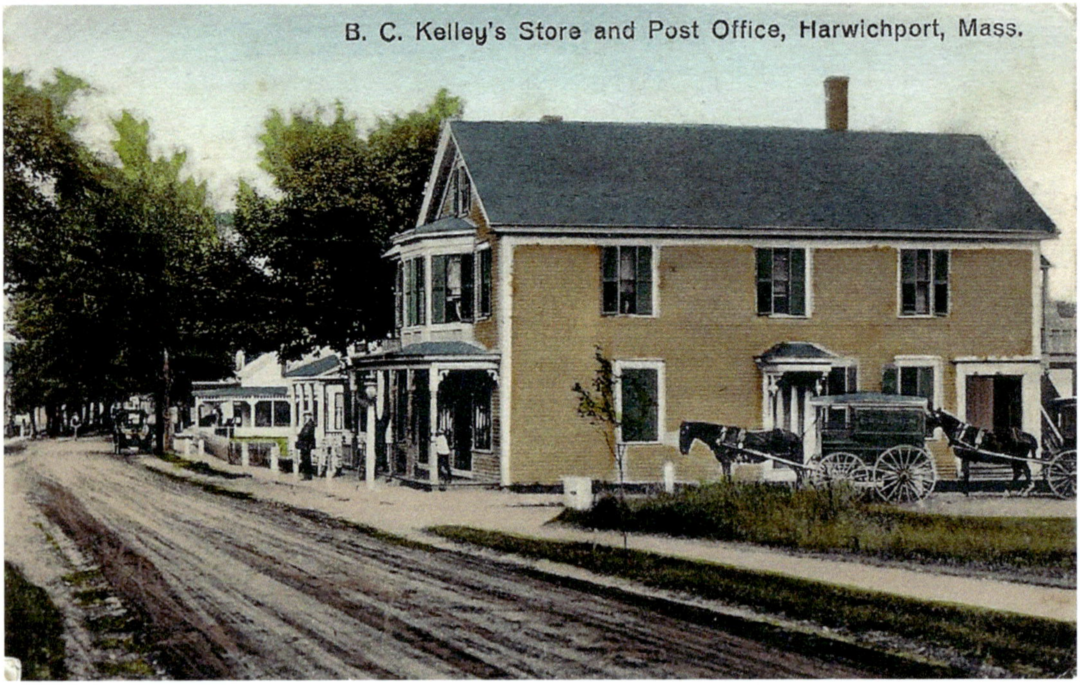

BUSIEST CROSSROAD: The corner where Sea and Main Streets meet was once the busiest in Harwich Port. B. C. Kelley's general store attracted shoppers, especially since it also housed the Port's post office. Sea Street led to the Kelley wharf and was the major thoroughfare carrying goods from arriving ships. Today the site is occupied by a popular restaurant.

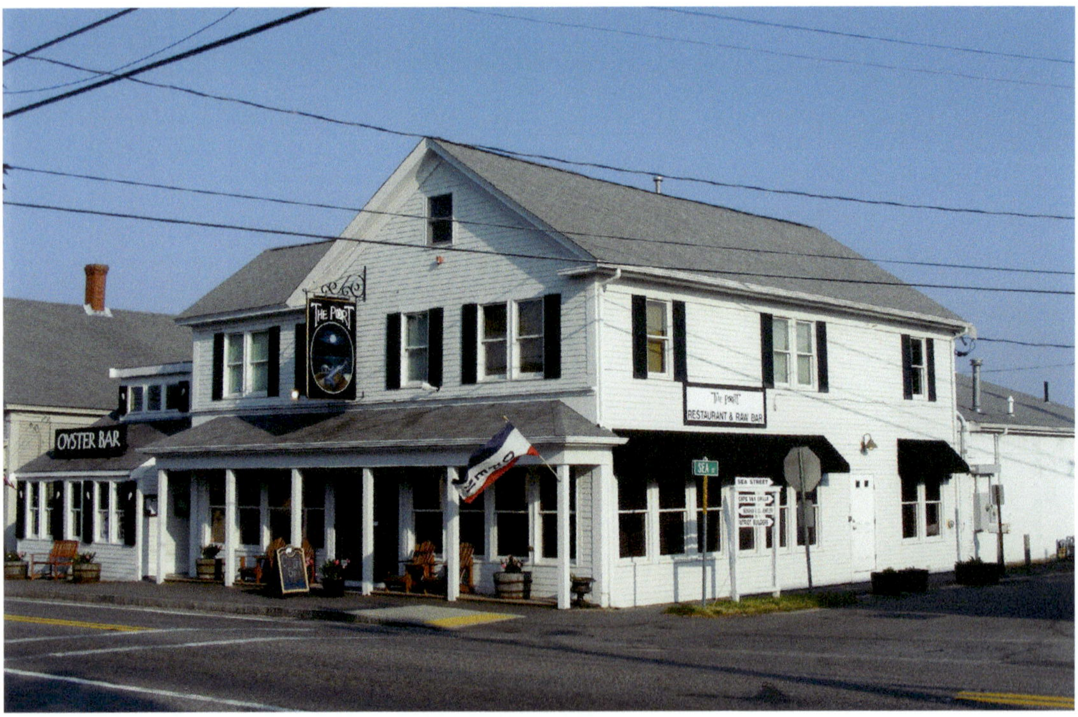

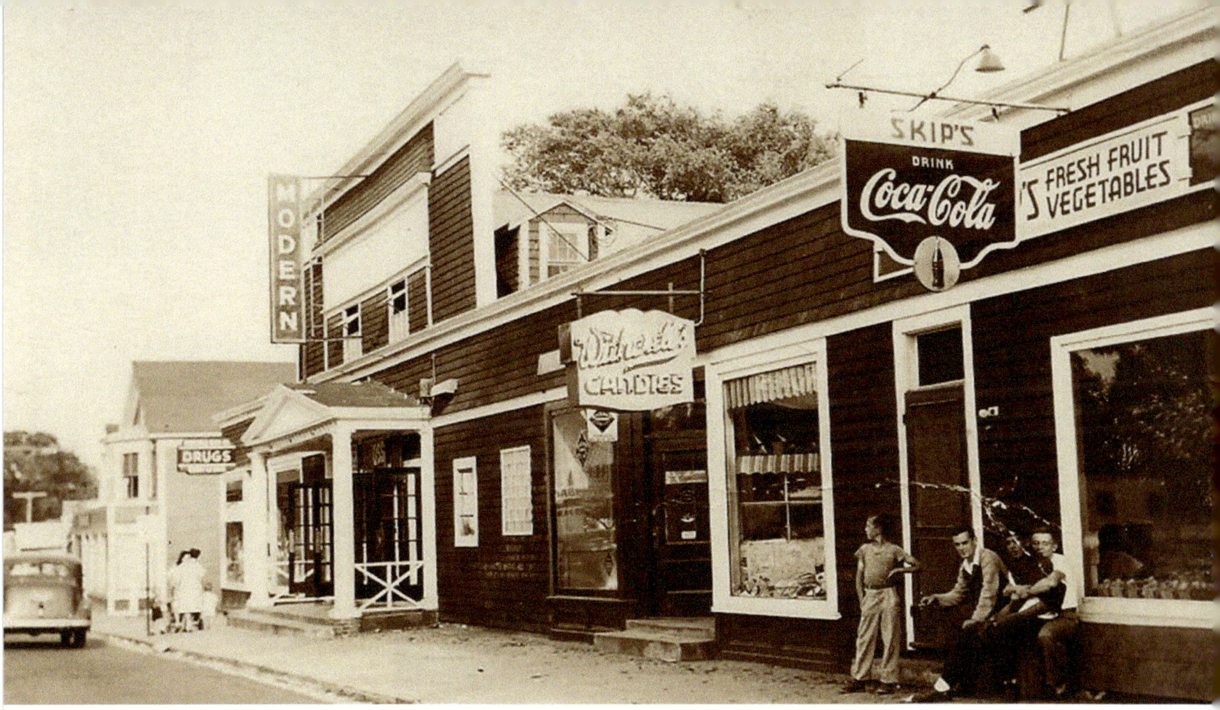

HARWICH'S FIRST MOVIE THEATRE: The Modern Theatre was built by Dr. Ginn on the eve of the First World War in a block of stores he owned. For fifteen cents a movie-goer could see two shows, while a five piece orchestra provided the mood music appropriate to the screen's action. Shows continued long after Ginn's failing health required him to sell the theatre. During the Second World War, pictures of local servicemen were flashed on the screen before the main feature. Bonatt's bakery and restaurant now occupy the space.

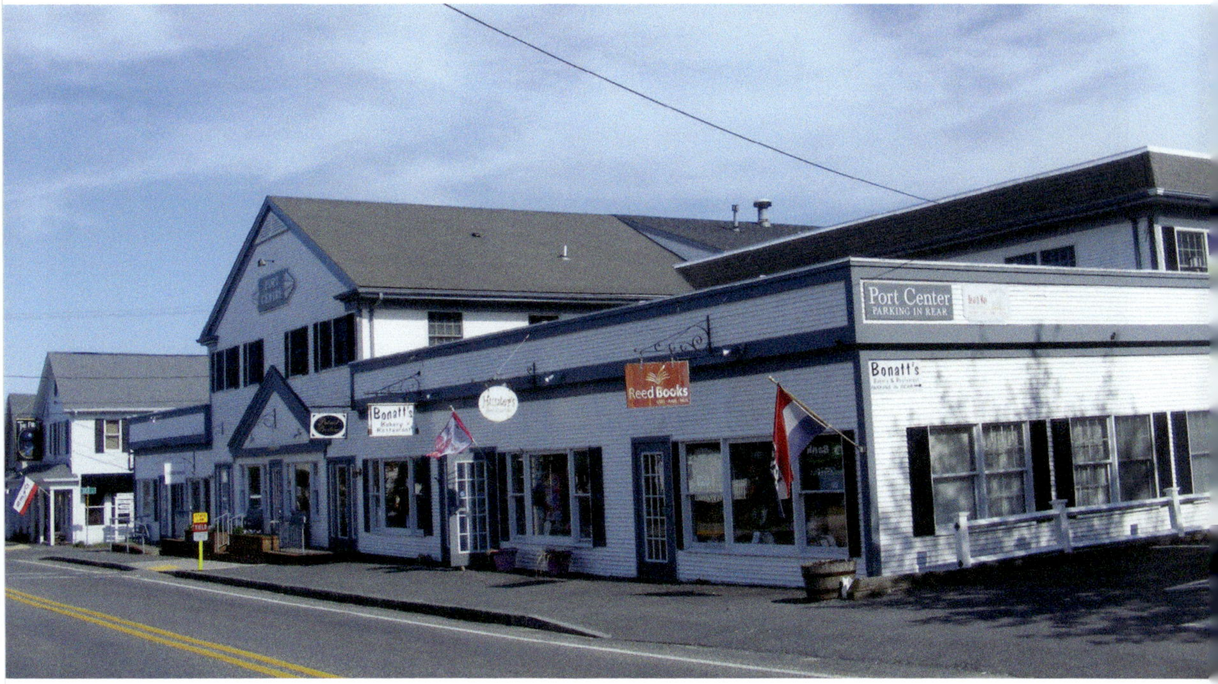

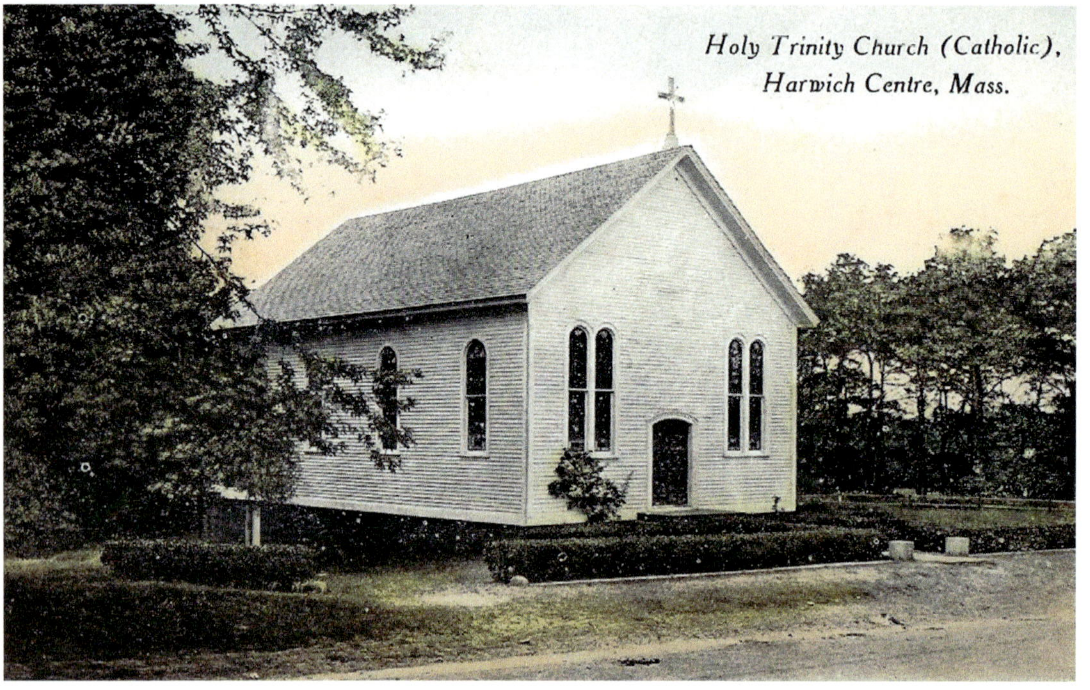

CATHOLIC CHURCHES: The first Catholic chapel in Harwich was built in 1865 in the Center, and destroyed by fire in 1927. Its successor, Holy Trinity, was built on Main Street at the West Harwich line: it also was destroyed by fire in 1963. This impressive church was erected on the same site. The latest addition is a small stone, medieval-style chapel visible in the background.

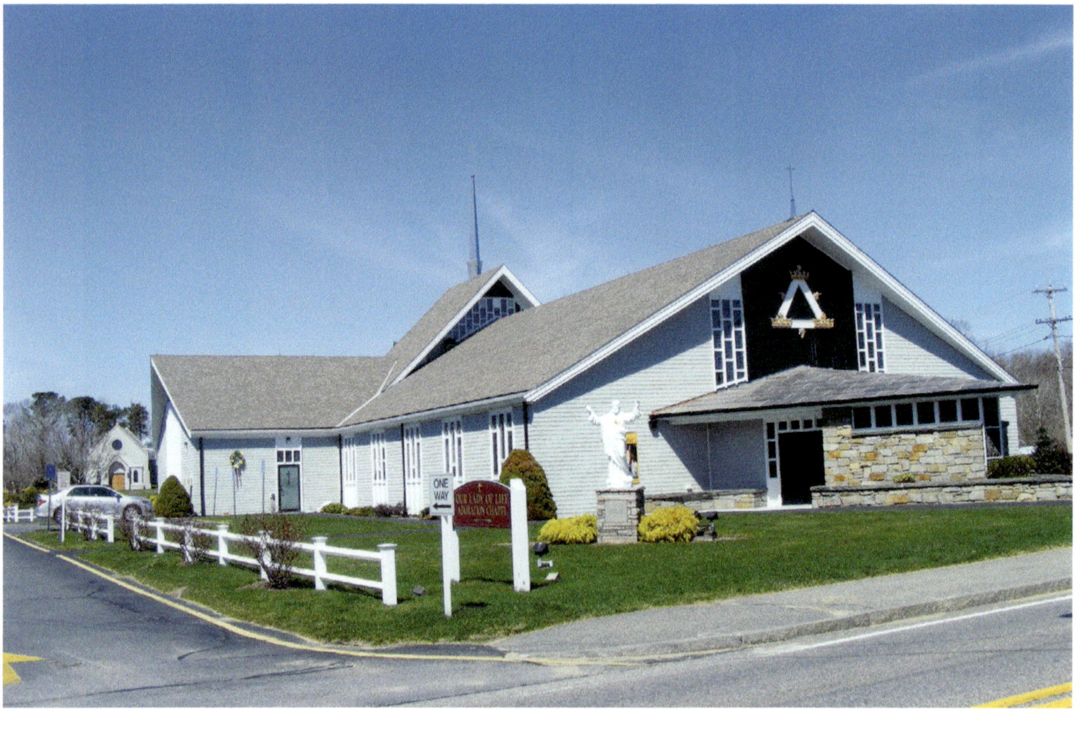

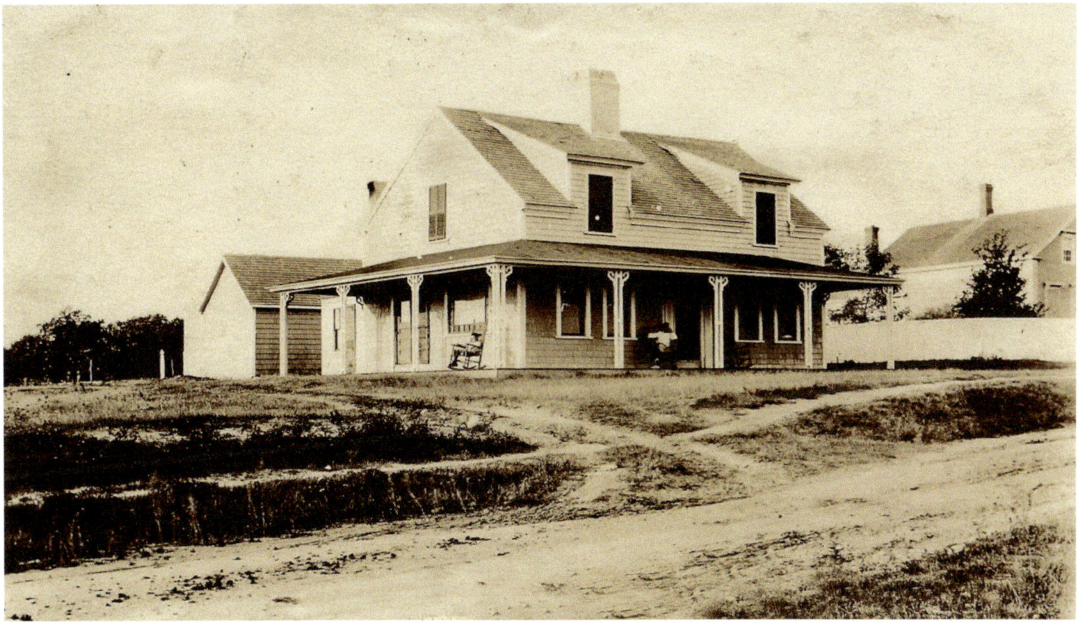

FIRST CHURCH OF CHRIST, SCIENTIST: Several local people met in the town library in 1954 to establish a Christian Science Society, acquire property, and build a church. They chose this lot high on a hill overlooking Wychmere Harbor and incorporated the existing house into the new facility. The church is now a branch of the First Church in Boston.

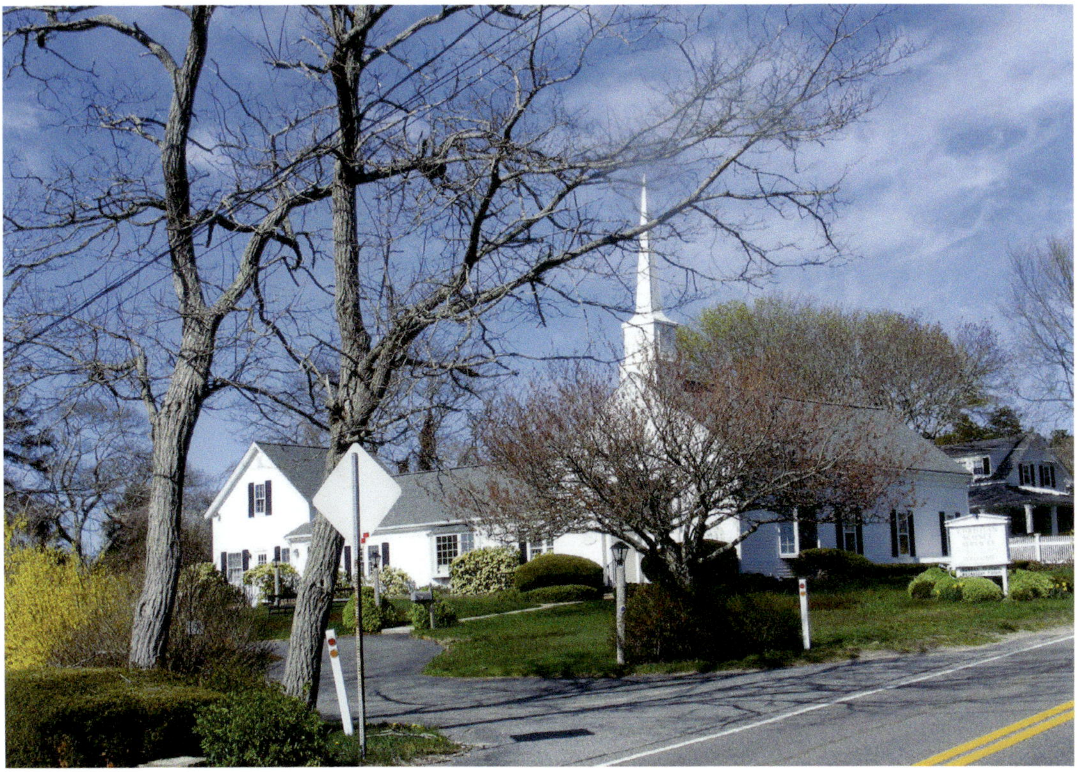

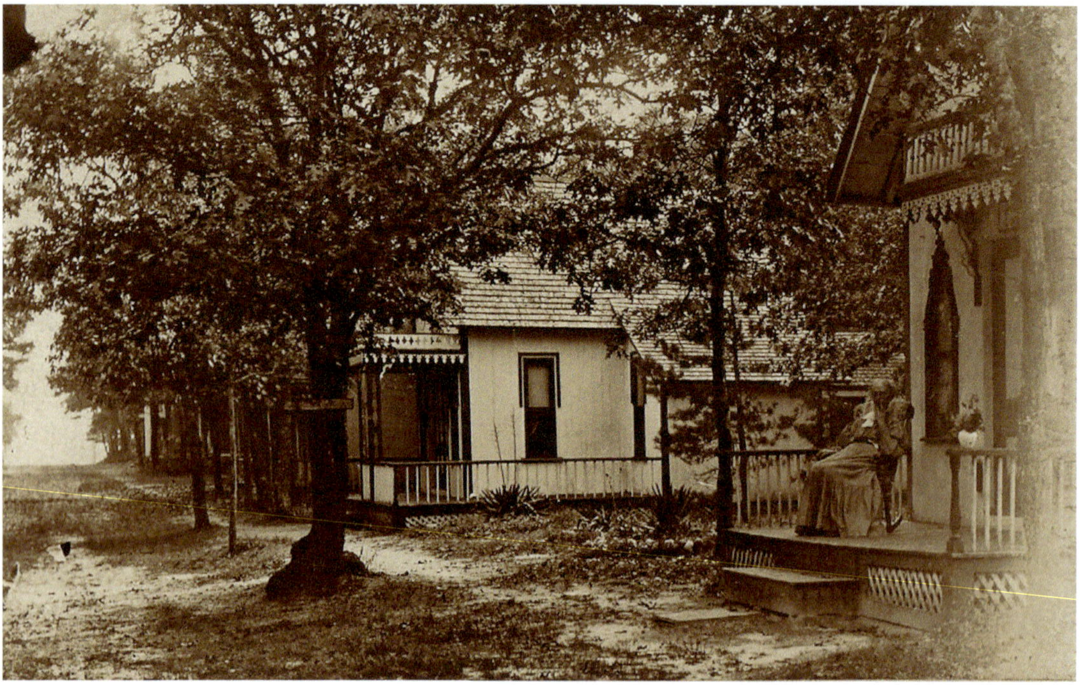

Camp Grounds: Ocean Grove, popularly called the Camp Grounds, was developed in the late nineteenth century to provide minimal housing for the large numbers of people who gathered there for open-air revival services. The narrow streets, small lots, and Victorian decorated homes later attracted persons seeking simple cottages near the beach. Many homeowners have preserved the original styles.

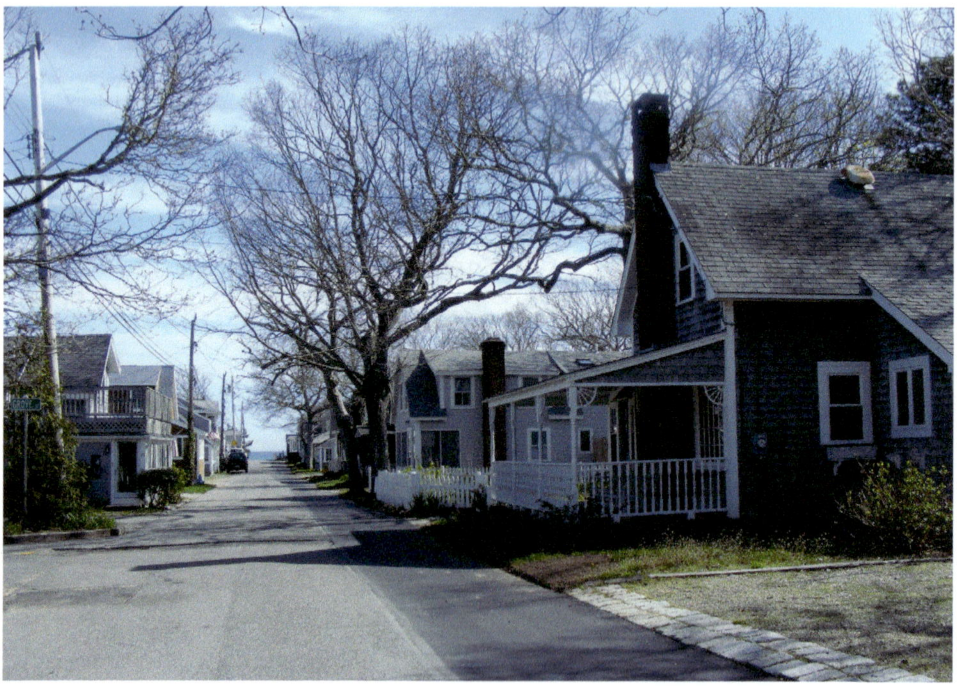

Methodist Meeting House:

The South Harwich Meeting House, built in 1836, blends elements of Greek and Gothic revival styles. Located on Chatham Road, it is listed with the National Register of Historic Places. After the congregation declined to a handful of members, the church merged with a church in East Harwich. In recent years, the town purchased the property and supporters raised funds for long overdue repairs. The meeting house's integrity has been restored, even to the two front doors that allowed women to enter by one and men through the other.

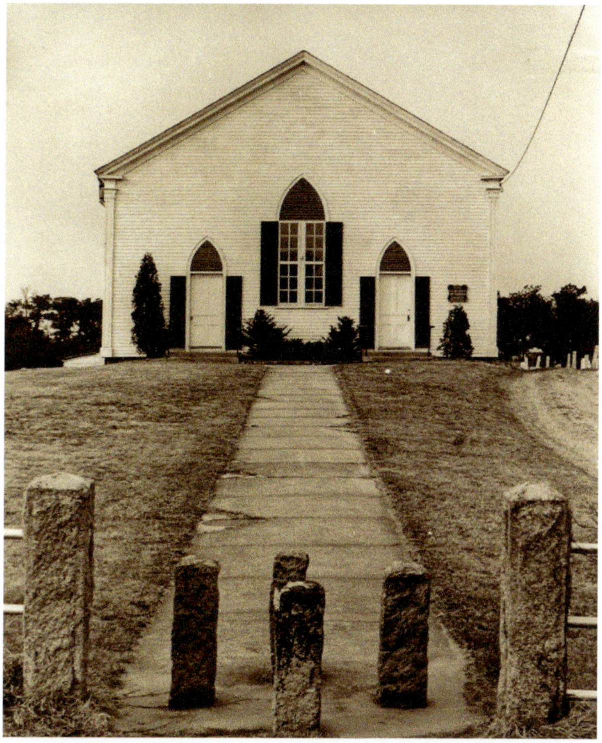

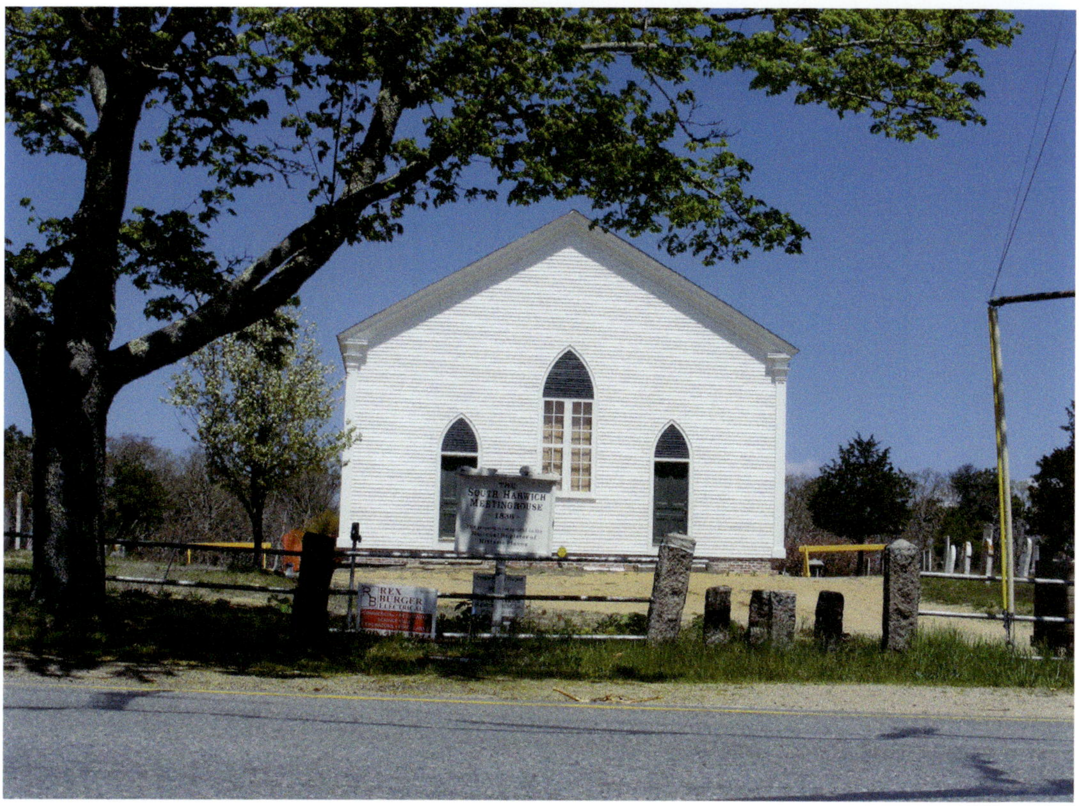

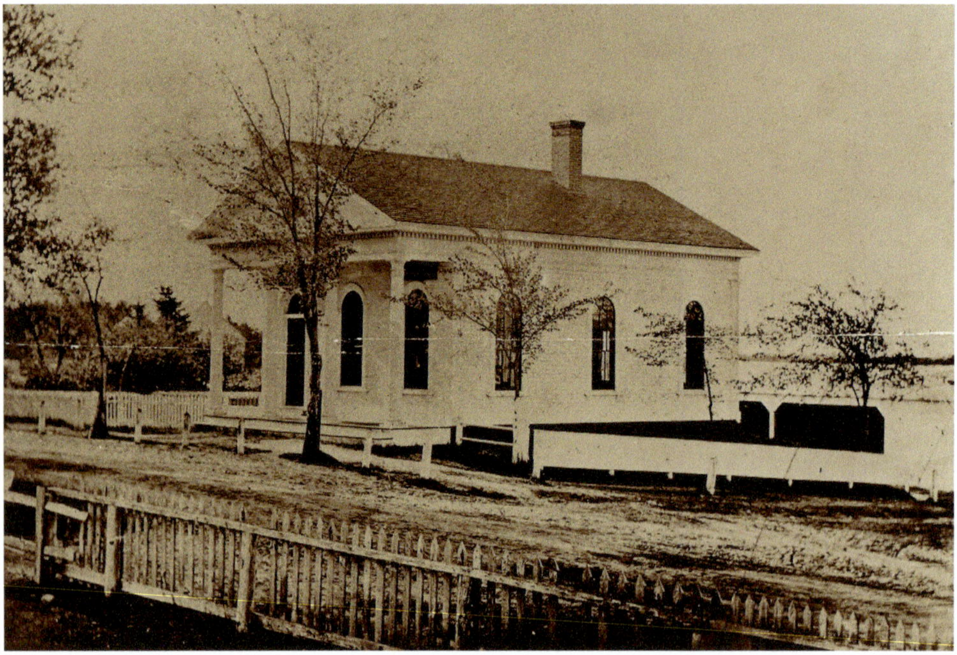

TOWN BANKS: The nearest bank was a stage coach trek away when several Harwich men petitioned the state legislature. In 1855, they were awarded two charters, since commercial banks did not then provide for personal accounts. A source of capital assured, investors were able to create a commercial hub. The Bank of Cape Cod and the Cape Cod Five shared this building on Main Street until the Five built its own facility in 1875. Look familiar? It is now the library's children's wing.

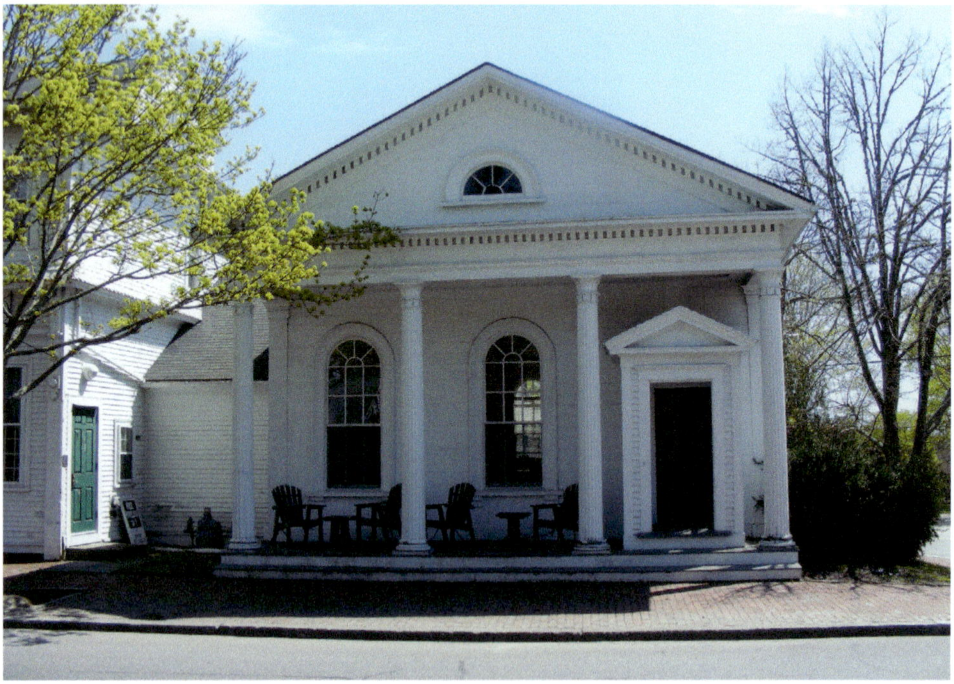

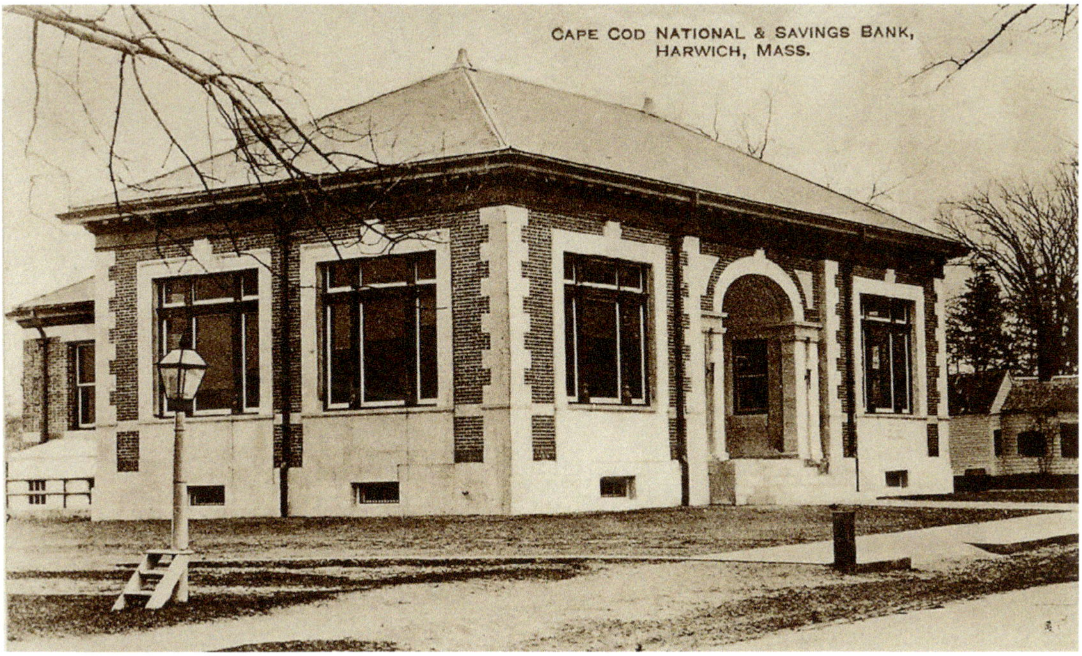

SHARED BANK FACILITIES: During the Civil War state-chartered banks were encouraged to become national banks. The renamed First National Bank of Cape Cod and the Five were reunited in this impressive brick and marble edifice built in 1914. When it became too small, the two banks built side-by-side quarters in Harwich Port. The Main Street building became the Harwich Town Offices.

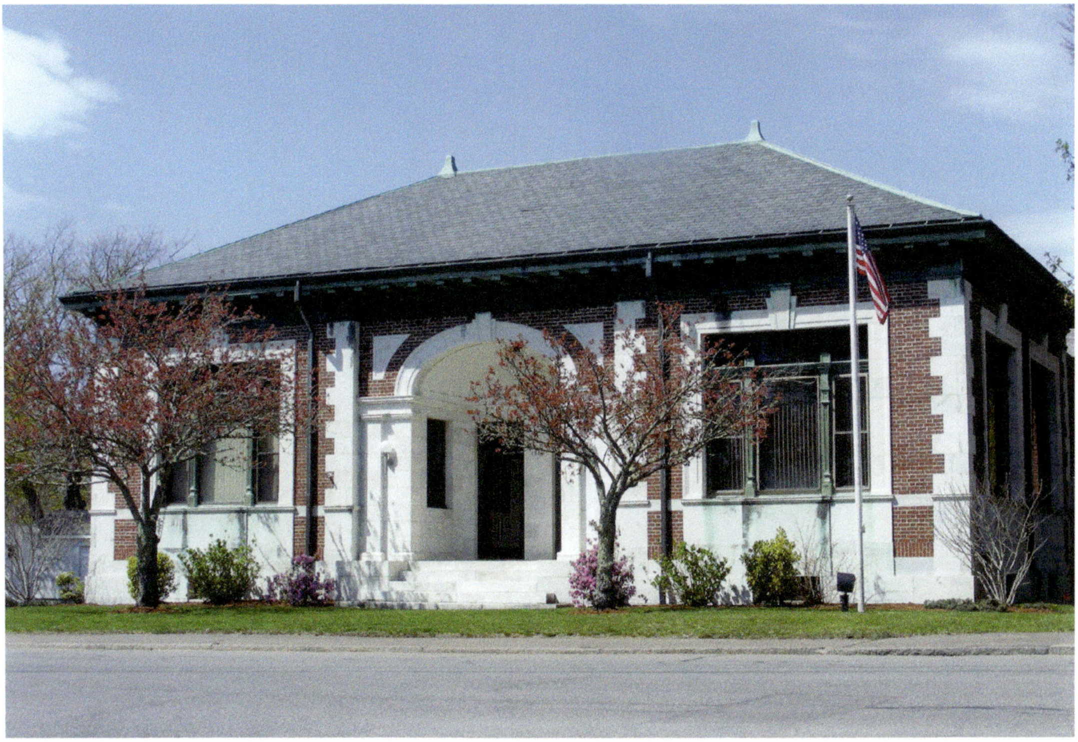

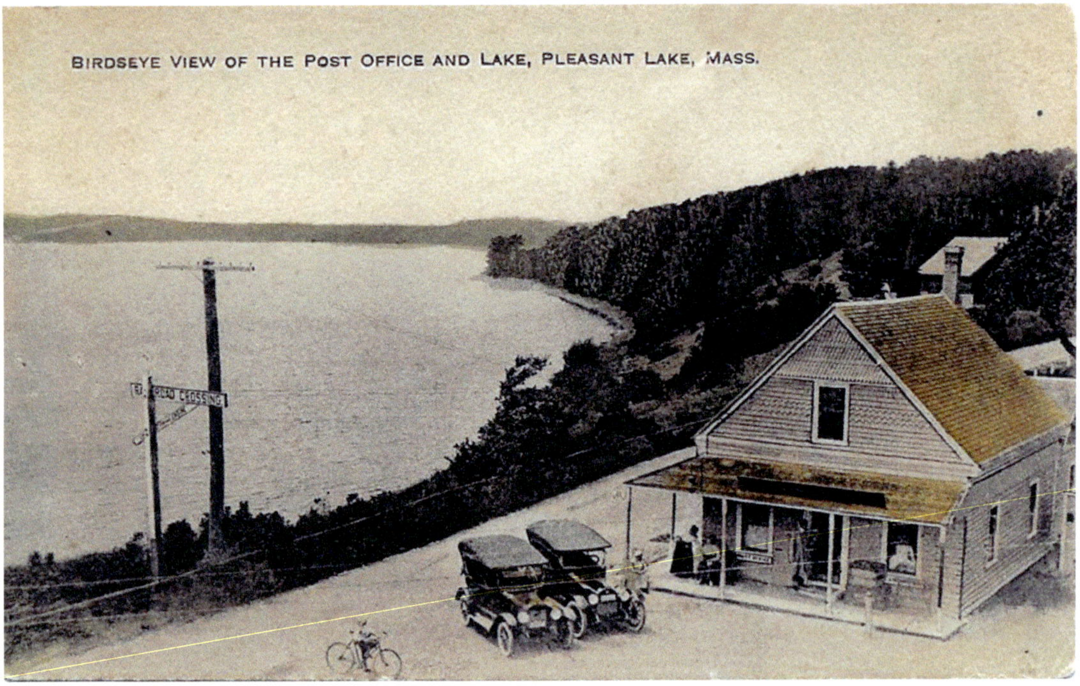

PLEASANT LAKE GENERAL STORE: Despite the rapid expansion of stores in Harwich Center, general stores continued to flourish in the villages. This one at Hinkley's Pond has been little changed over the last century. Much of its trade today comes from cyclists who use the adjacent bike path. Note the restrictions on use of the benches.

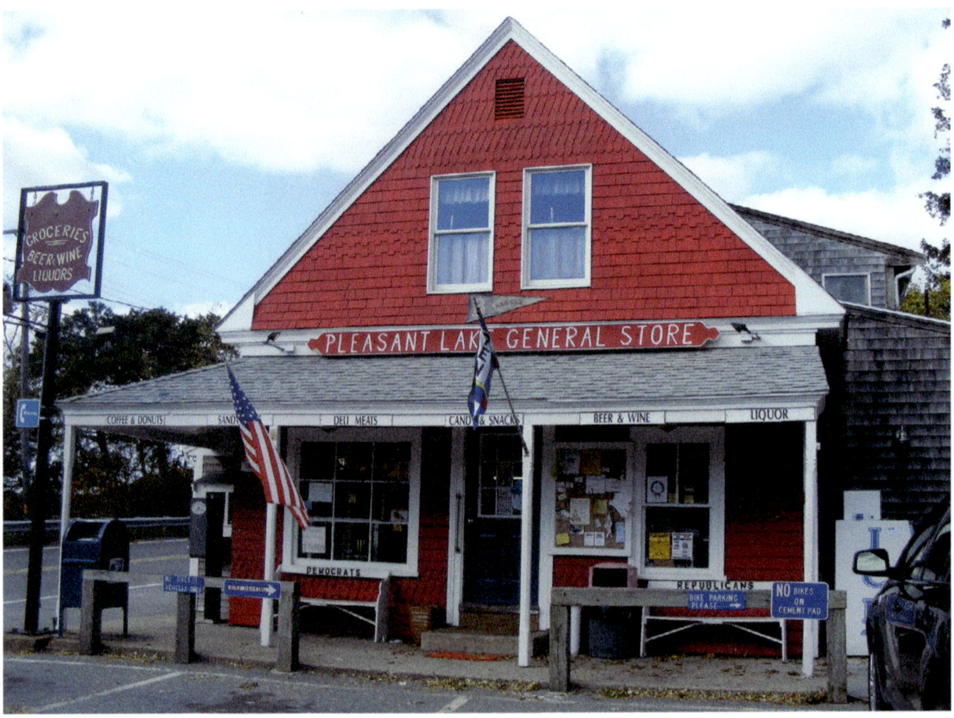

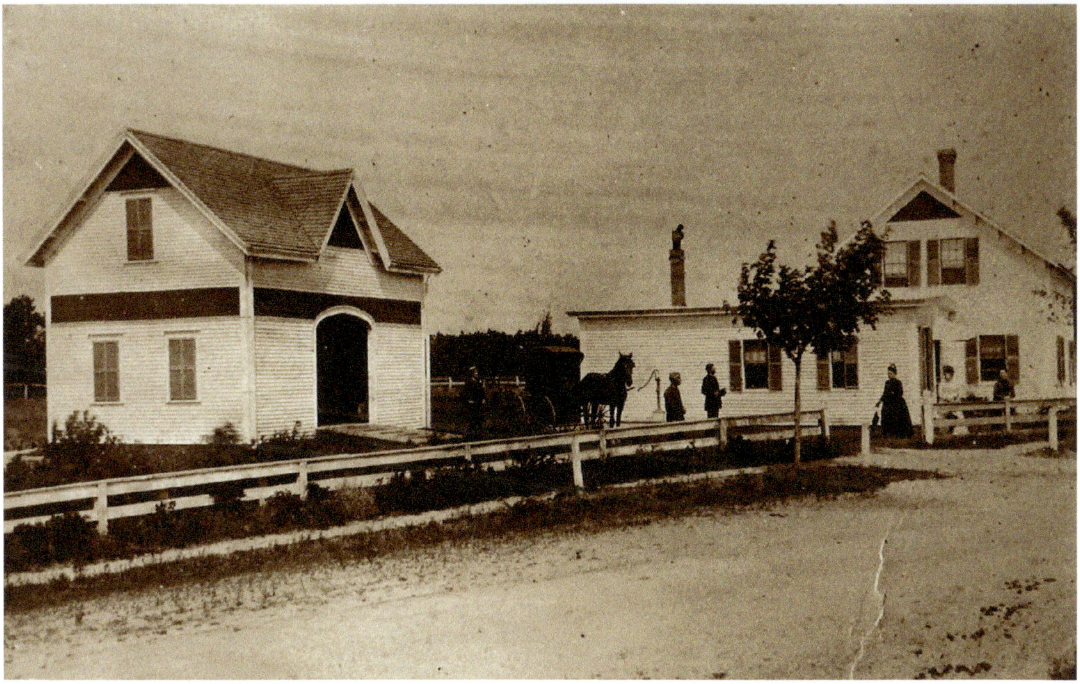

SOUTH HARWICH STORE: A general store at the intersection of the Chatham and Old County Roads provided for the local community in rooms in the elongated extension between house and barn. The house today is a private residence in the process of being painstakingly preserved.

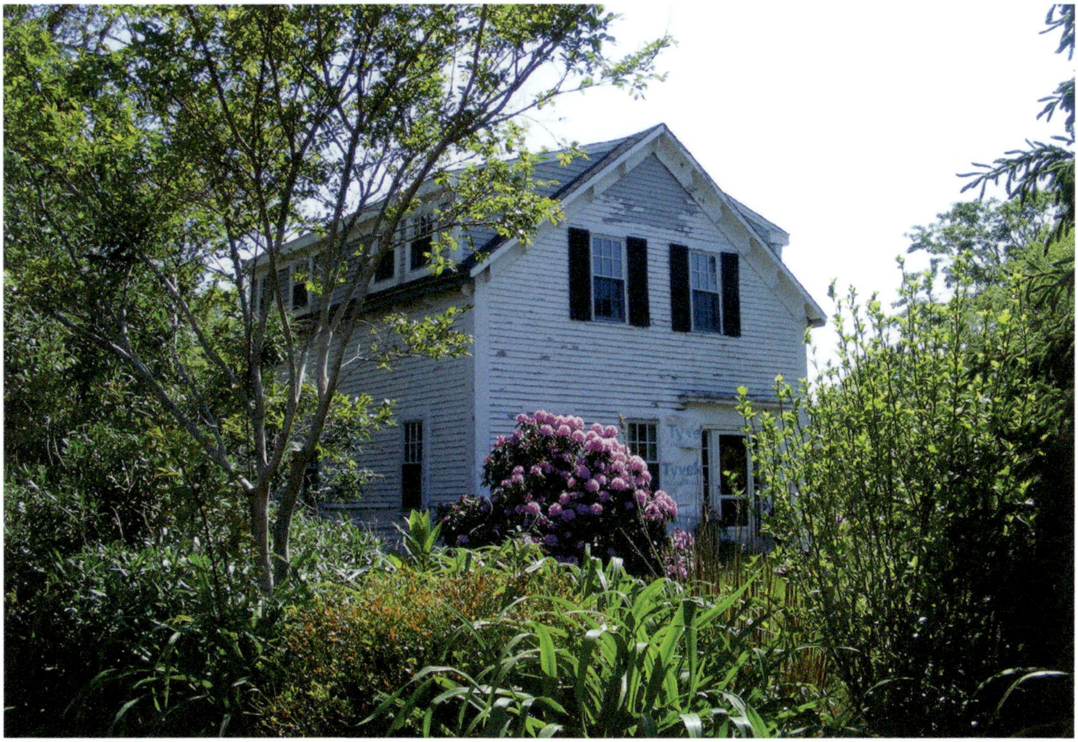

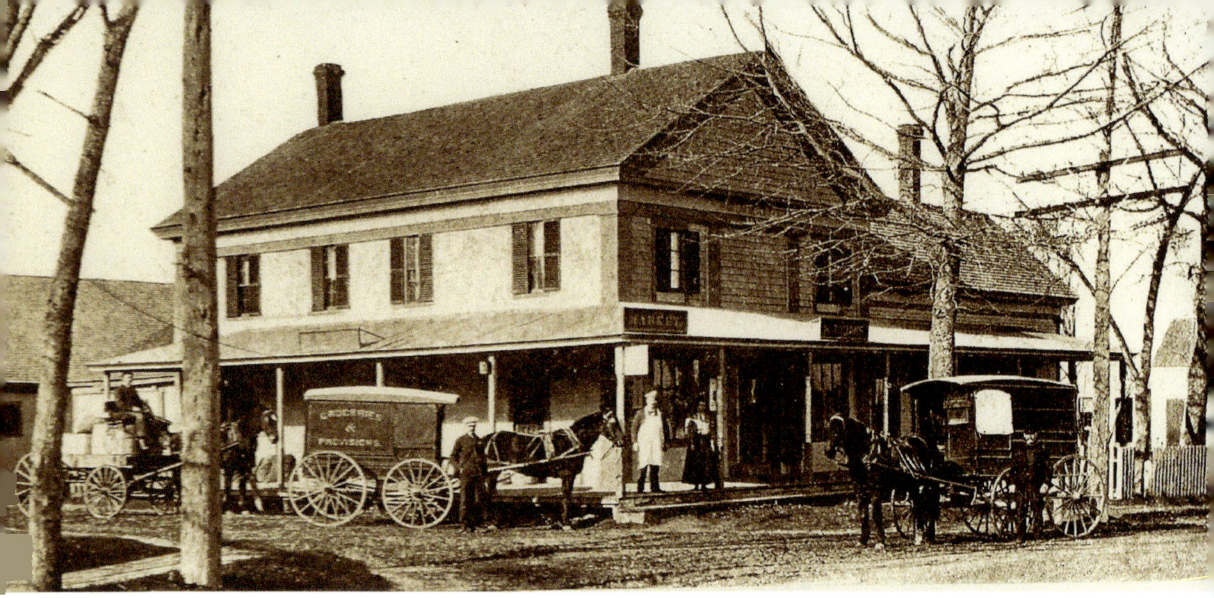

UNION HALL STORE: At the corner of Bank and Miles Streets in Harwich Port, this general store had a large public hall on the second floor for meetings and socials. The ground floor facilities offered a wide variety of goods. In recent years this building has been converted into multiple unit housing.

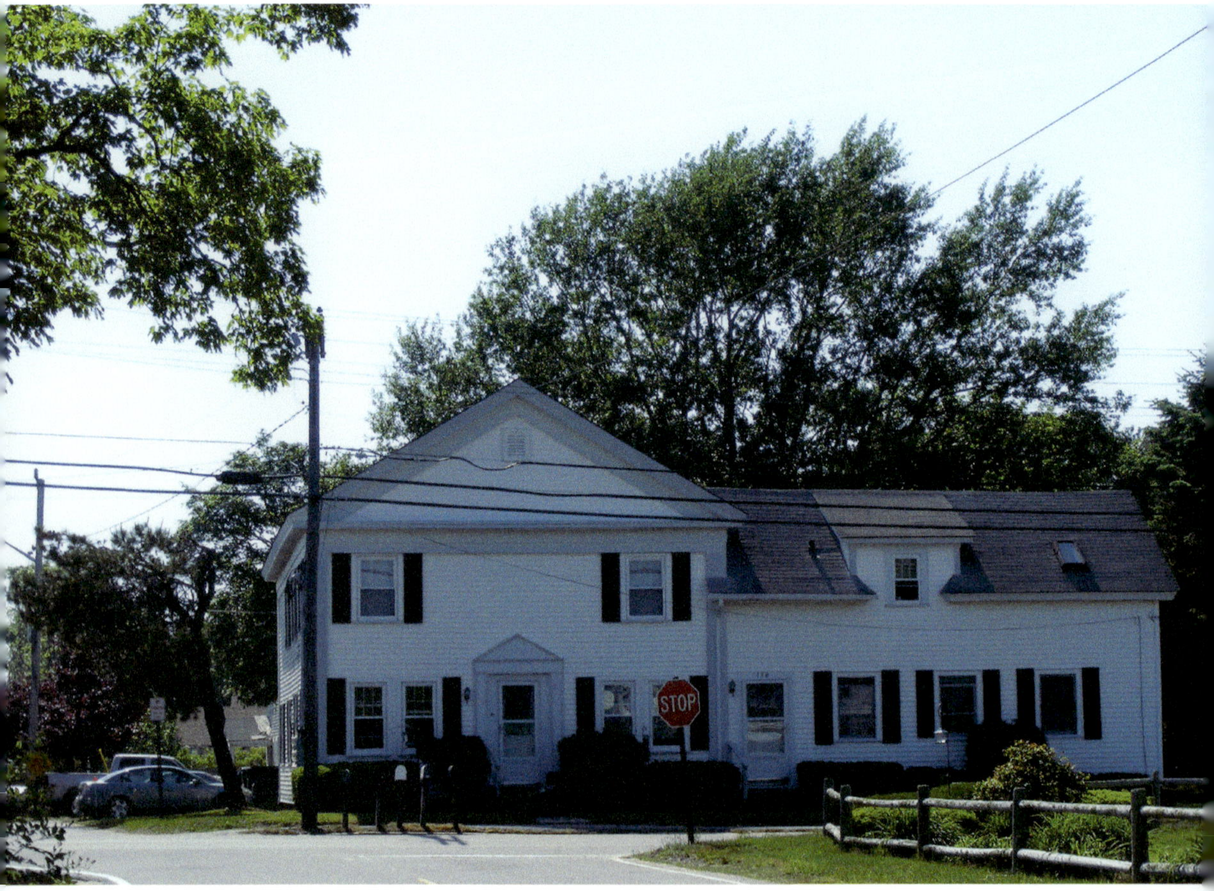

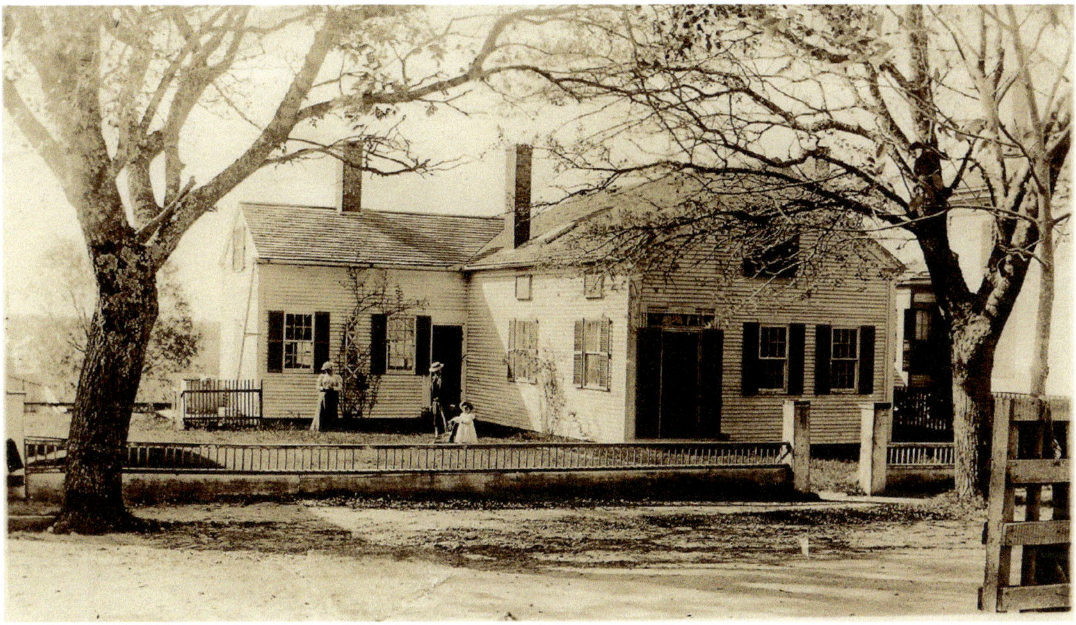

THACHER'S FORGE: The blacksmith performed many essential services. Solomon Thacher's forge behind his residence in the town Center was the busiest of the three operating in 1860. Thacher was an original investor in the Savings Bank and a founding subscriber for Pine Grove Seminary. His forge eventually became an antique store, but is now vacant. A gas station uses part of the house as its office.

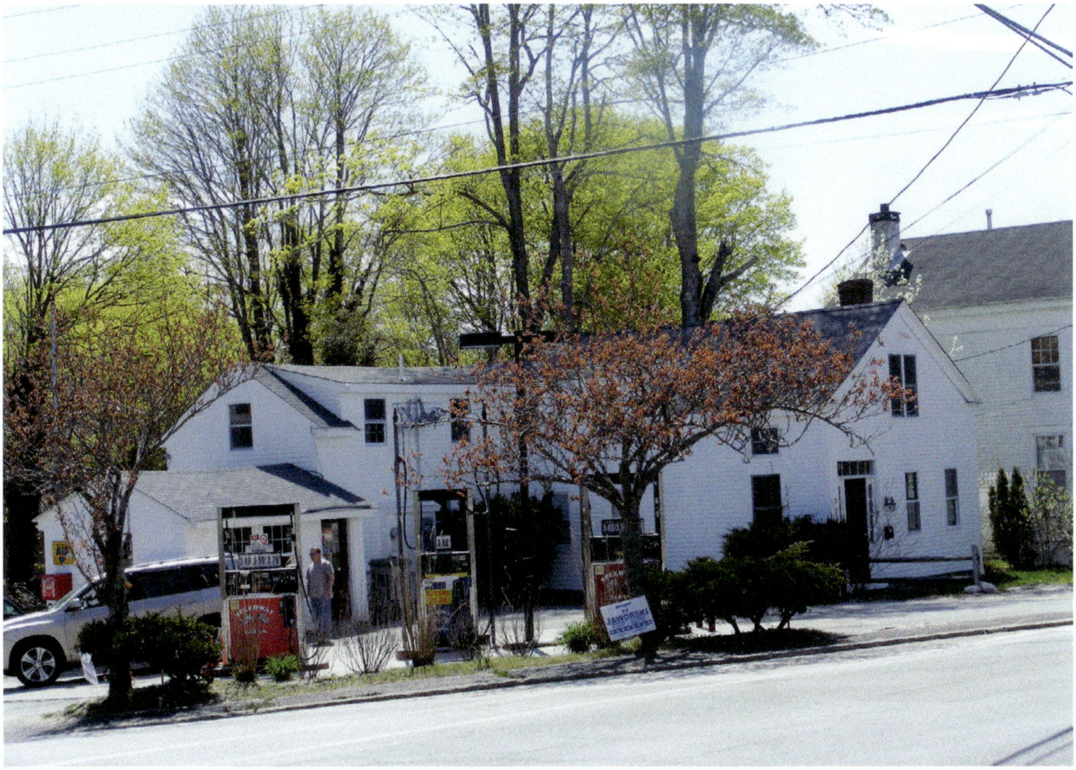

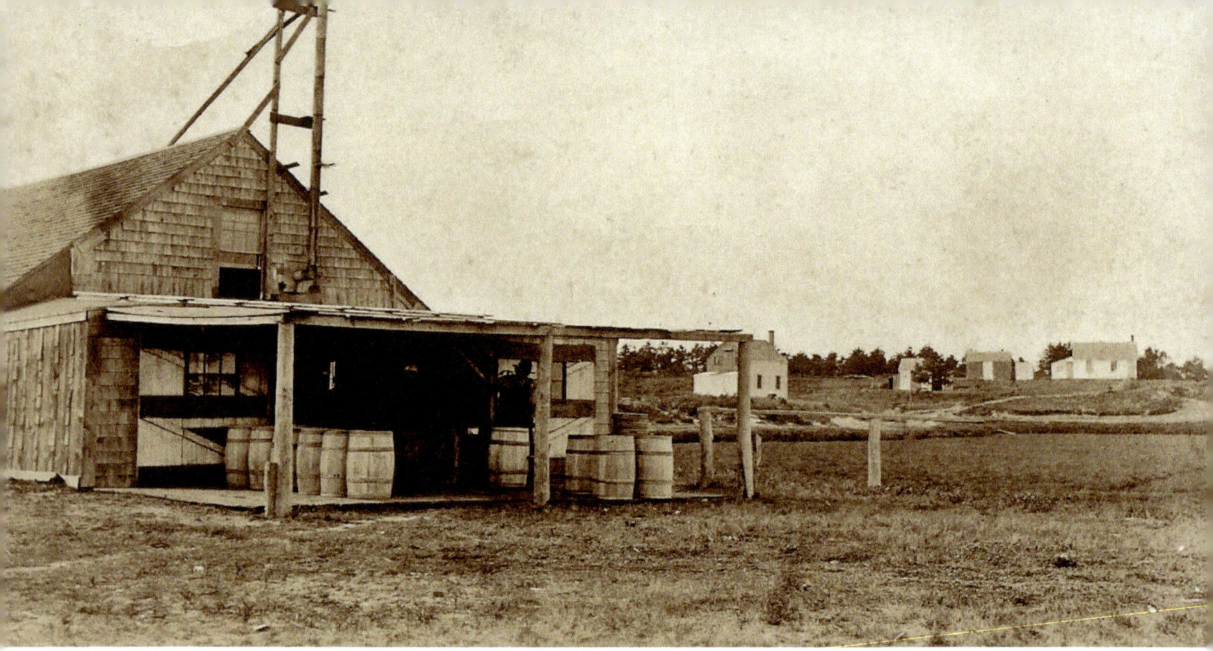

BARREL MAKING: Barrels were once vital for storing and transporting fish, and then for the cranberry crop. Wooden crates eventually were preferred for ease of handling and barrel manufacturing is becoming a lost art. One enterprising person has successfully converted an East Harwich barrel factory into production of beach chairs and rental of kayaks.

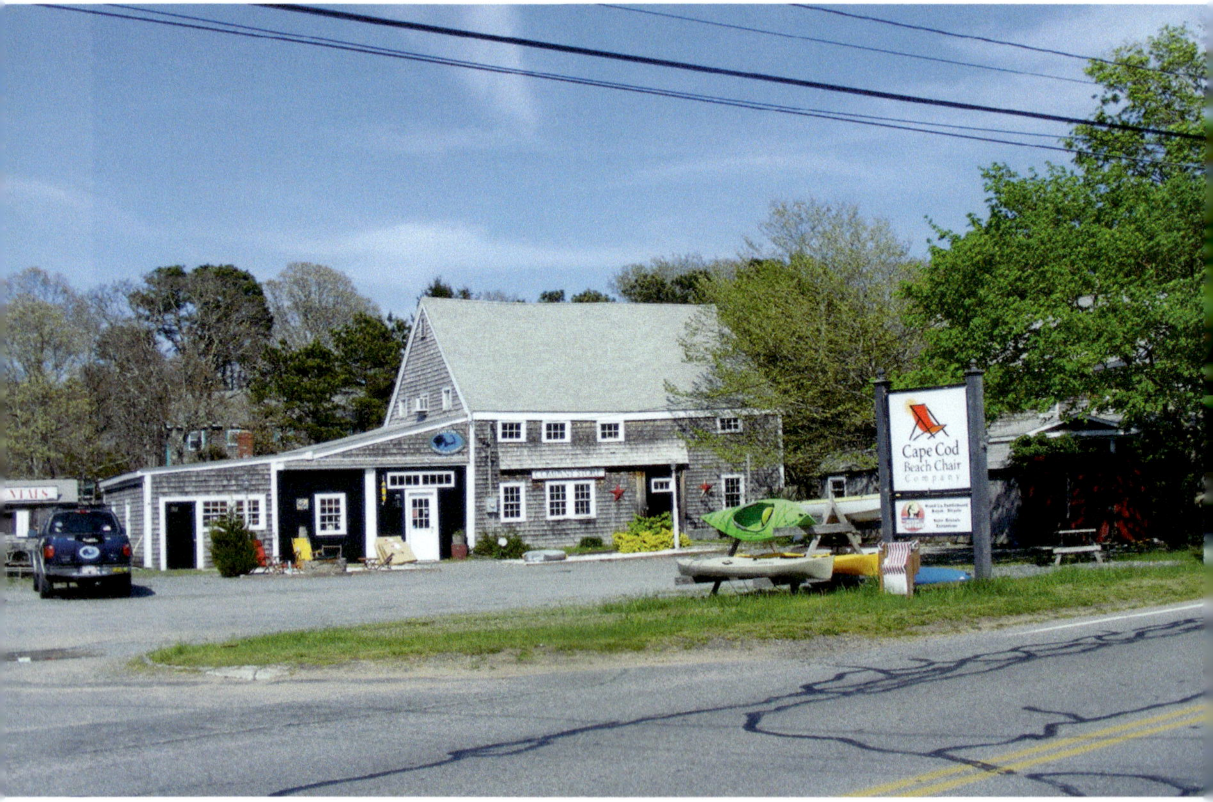

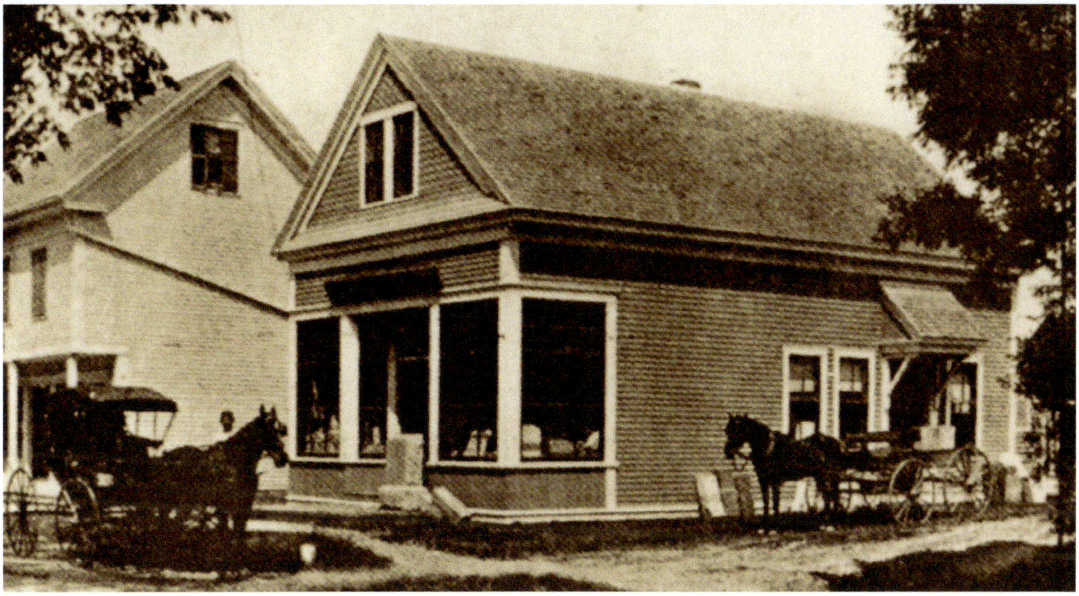

CROSBY MONUMENTS: This shop has served the community in its location next to the Congregational Cemetery since it was founded in the early 1870s. Henry Crosby, born in Orleans, learned his skills off Cape before selecting Harwich for his business and residence. Peter Blute, the current owner, has continued Crosby's tradition of the highest craftsmanship and service.

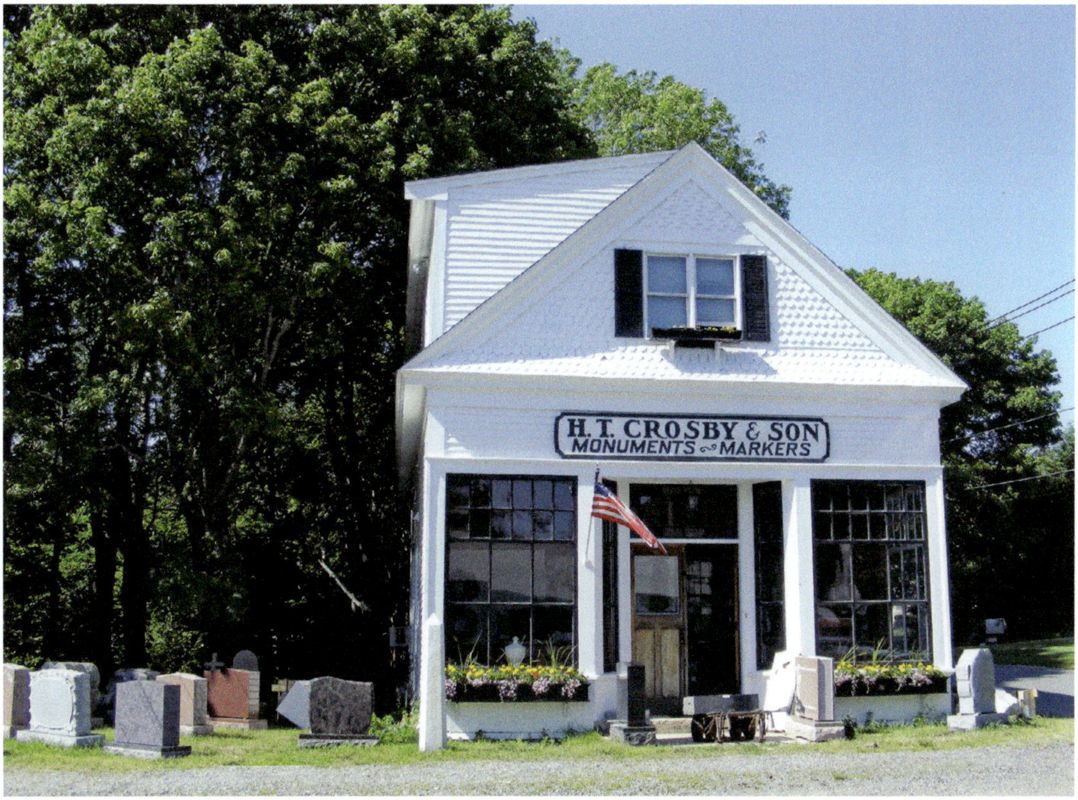

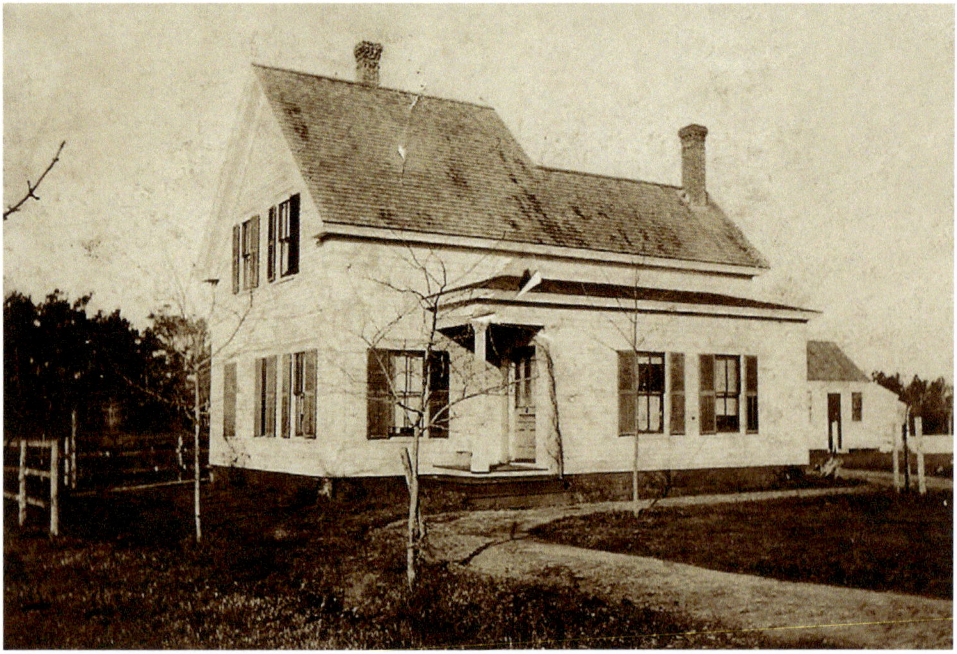

THE HARWICH UNDERTAKER: The town undertaker held a place as respected as it was essential. Asa Jones was born in Harwich, became a hero in the Civil War commanding a unit of the 6th Colored Infantry, and was later rewarded with appointment as keeper of the Monomoy Lighthouse. Jones returned to this comfortable home on Oak Street to raise his family. He conducted his undertaking business from an outbuilding and kept his hearse in a town barn. Today the home is a private residence.

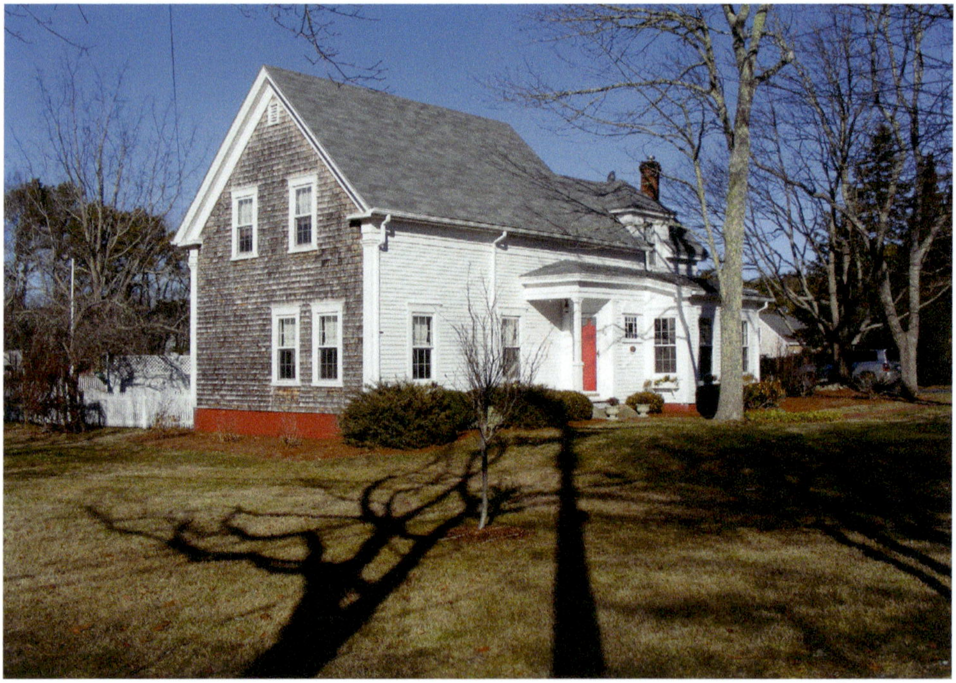

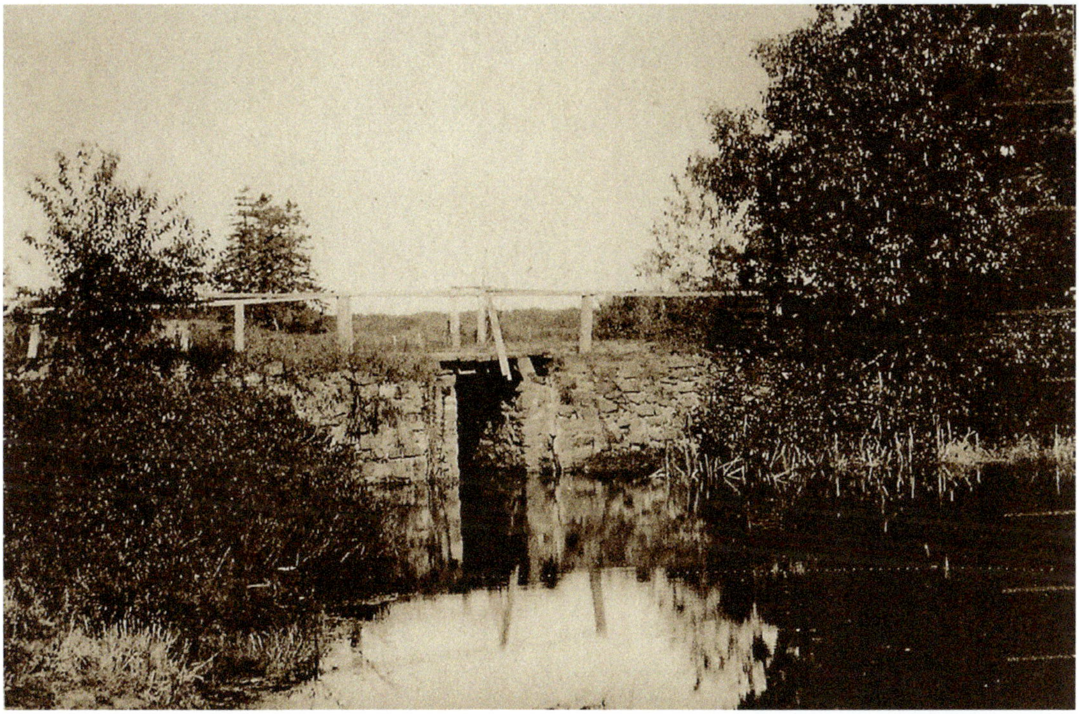

The Cotton Factory:

Manufacturing was slow to get a foothold locally. Lacking a significant source of water power, several local investors tried to use available sites. In this case, the Andrews River, which empties into Saquatucket Harbor in Harwich Port, was chosen to open a cotton-carding factory in the 1820s. It failed within a few years. Only vestiges remain, such as this small bridge over the stream.

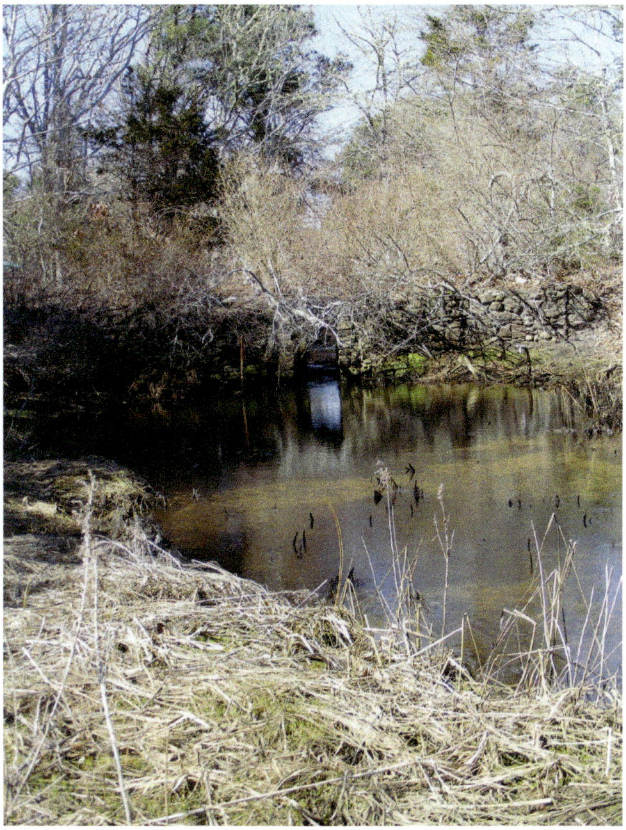

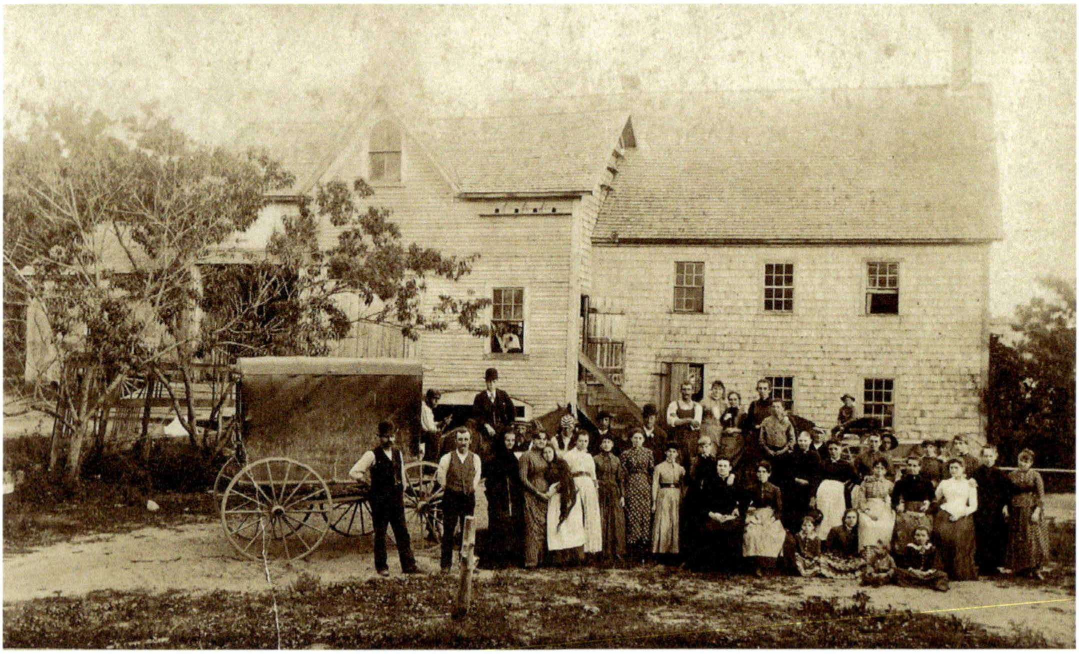

THE OVERALL FACTORY: The first successful factory in Harwich was built after the Civil War. A tiny, but determined woman was pregnant and caring for a three year old when her husband was lost at sea and her house faced foreclosure. Hannah Stokes built an overall factory on her property in South Harwich that gave employment to several hundred in the community. Her home was the building to the left. It was remodeled and enlarged in 1920 and is a private residence.

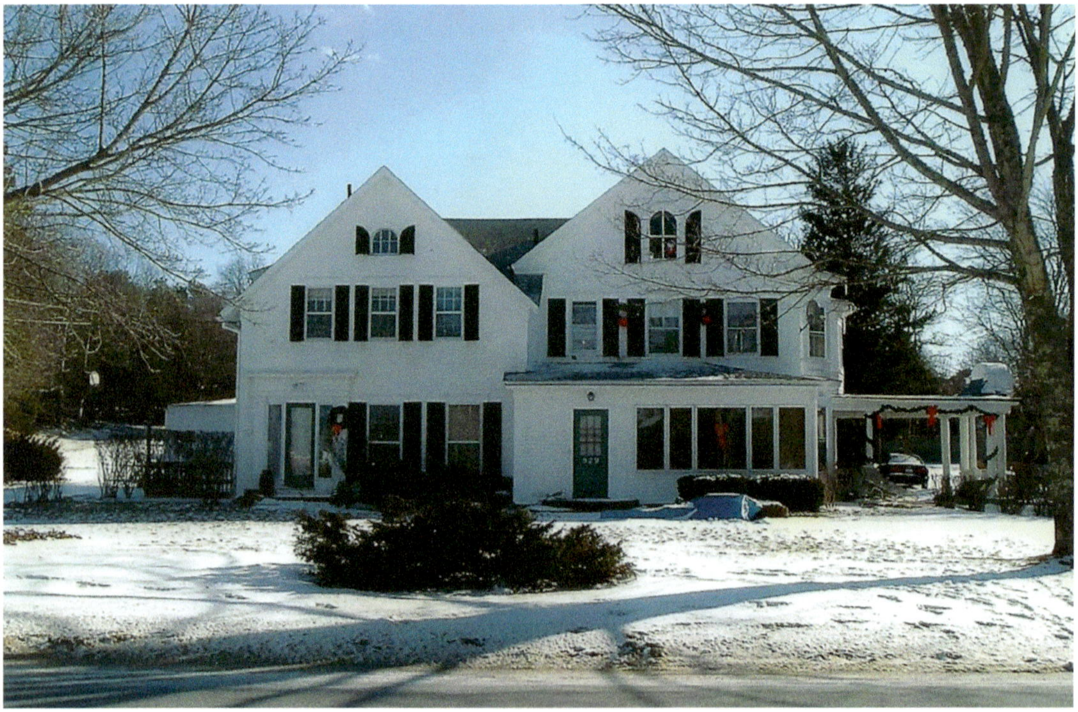

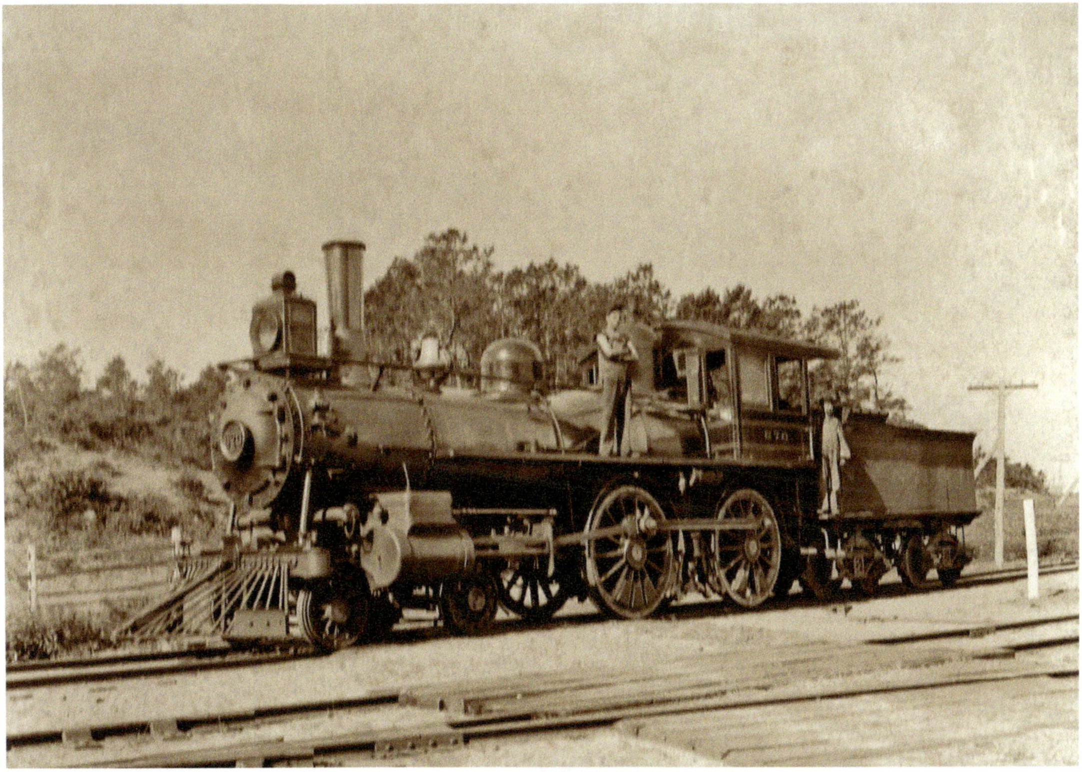

Impact of the Railroad:

The first train arriving in Harwich was greeted with wild enthusiasm in 1865. The line from Middleboro, through Sandwich, and eventually to Provincetown not only linked the Cape's towns to one another but also to the bigger world beyond. Dreamers imagined fortunes to be made by export. In reality, fortunes would be made by "import" – of tourists seeking accommodations. The impact continues in a different way: the rail beds have been converted to well-used bike paths.

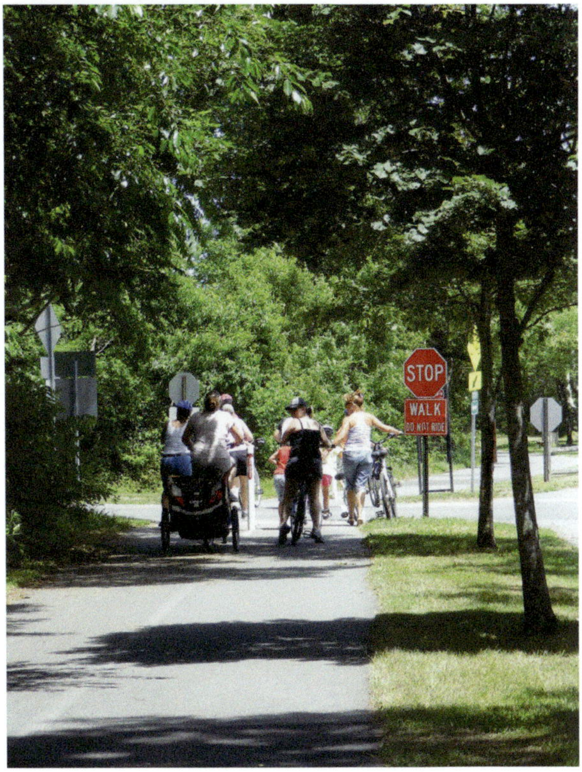

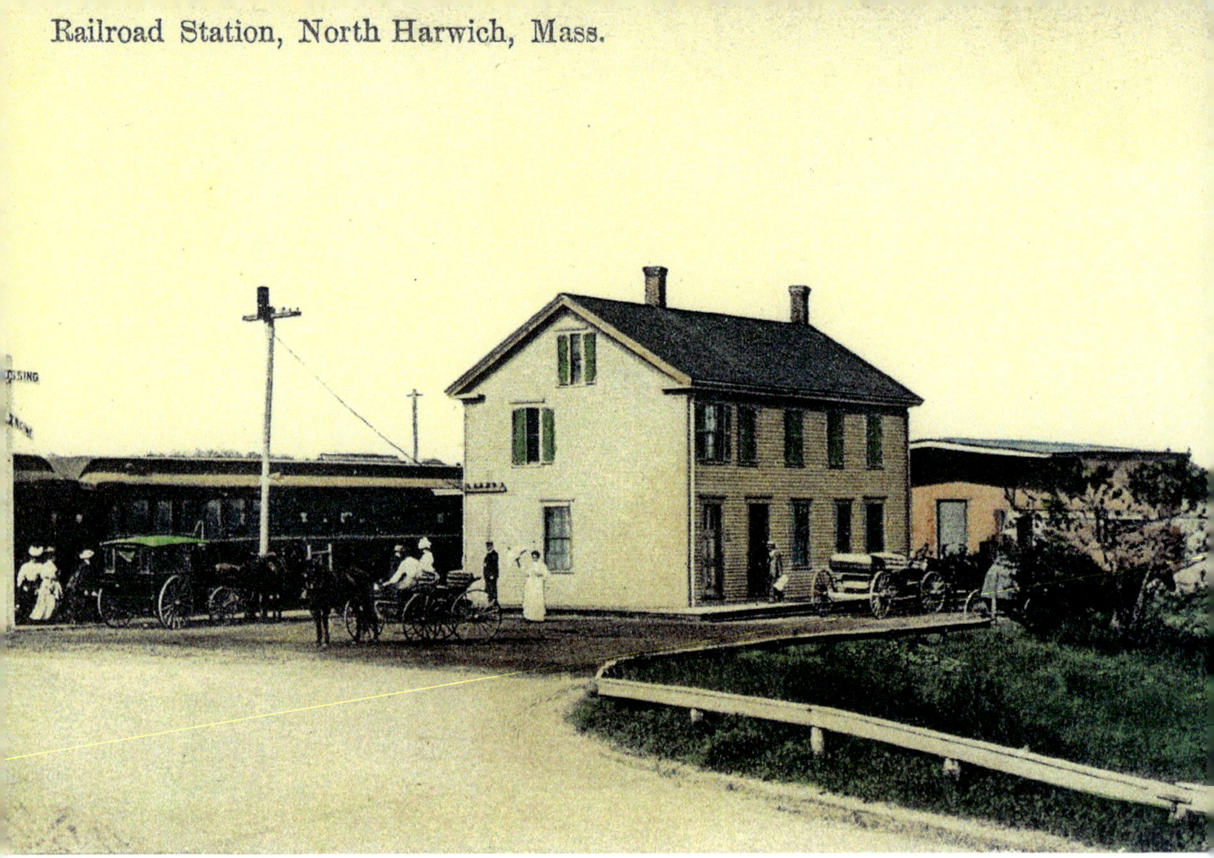

HARWICH STATIONS: Railroad stations were built in several of the villages and flag-down stops were made in others. The Harwich Center station also offered connections to Chatham by the 1870s. Both stations provided livery service for arriving passengers. The North Harwich station became the main stop for delivery of freight and storage facilities grew around it. Today the North Harwich station is being revitalized as the Olde Depot Industrial Park.

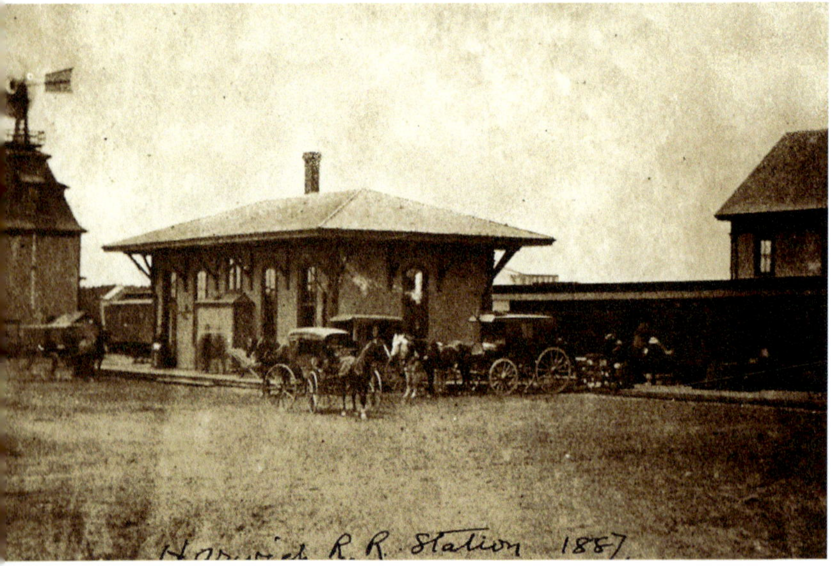

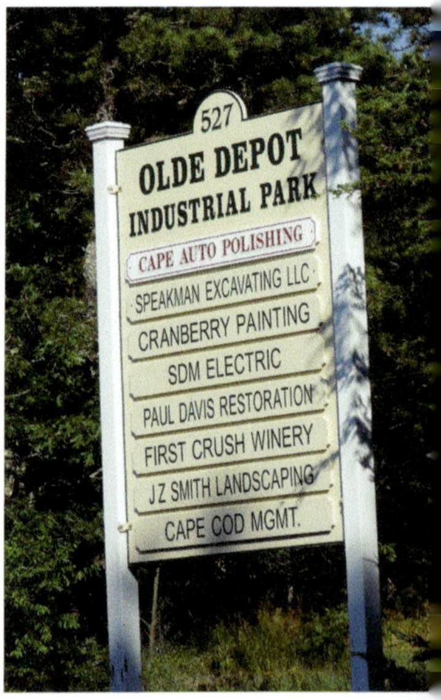

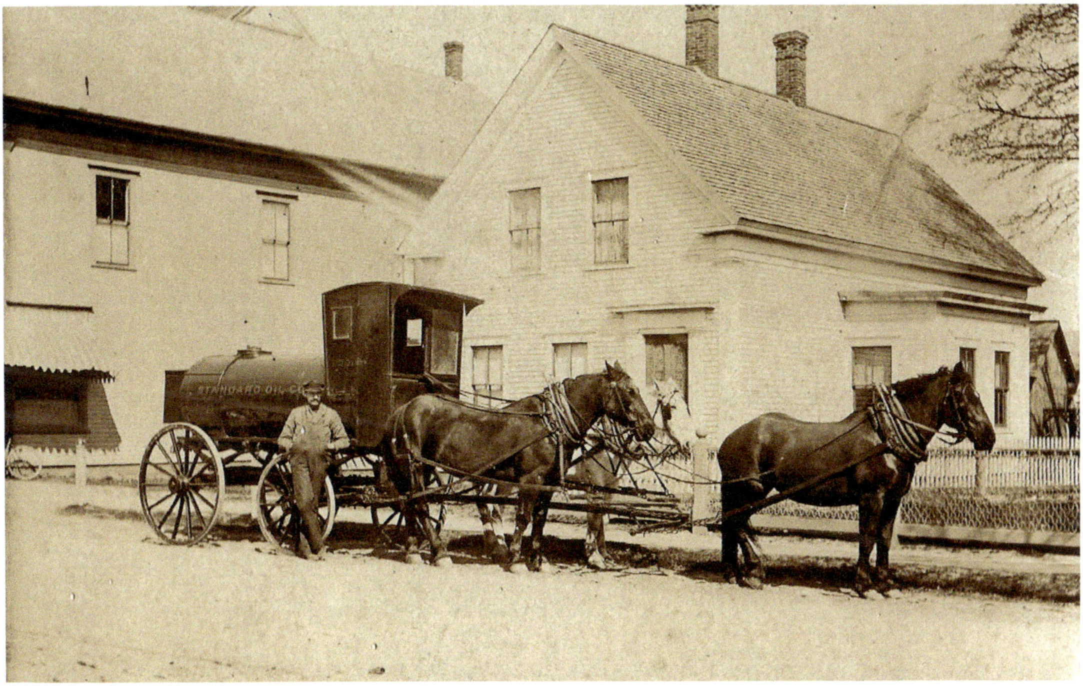

CHANGES IN 'HORSEPOWER': Mass production made the automobile available to the general public and forever changed transportation. The earlier photograph shows a three horse-team needed to pull the oil tank for deliveries. The horses would be replaced by a gasoline-powered truck.

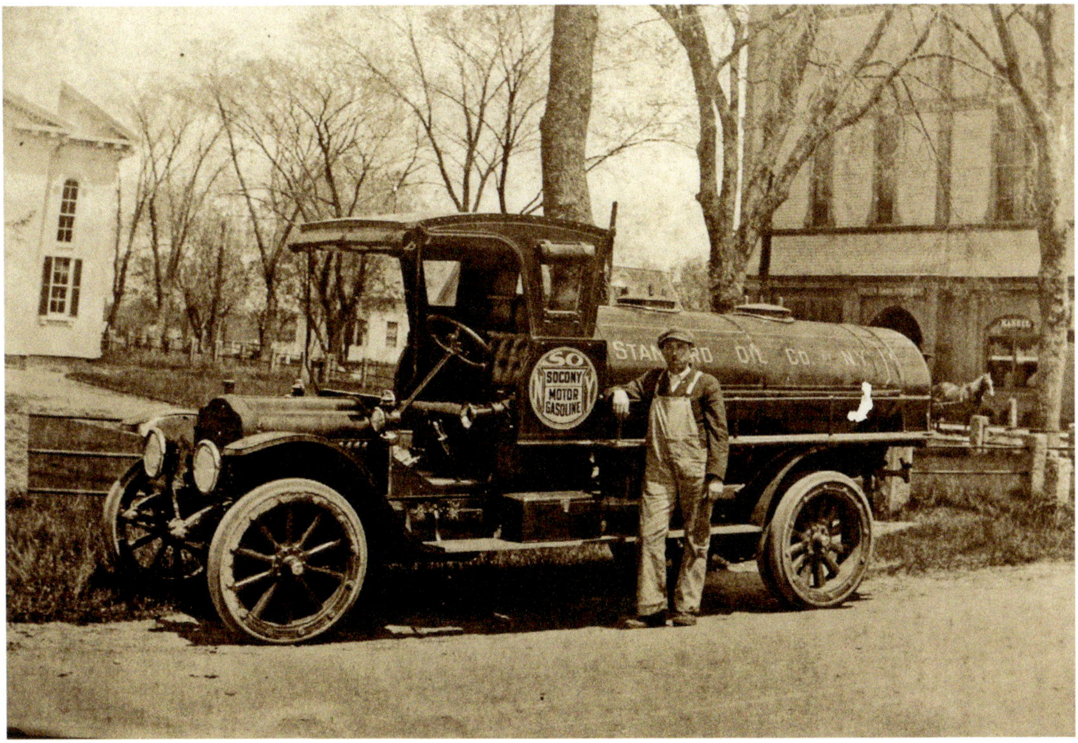

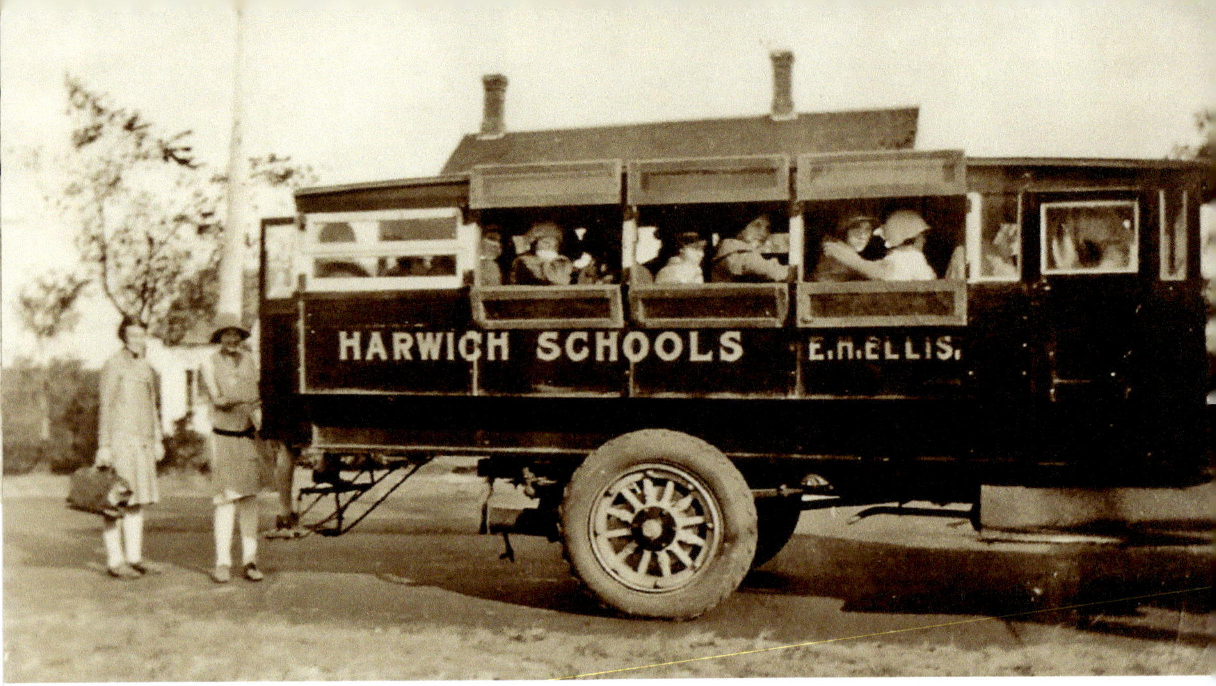

SCHOOL BUSES: Harwich introduced this bus early to provide for students who lived substantial distances from the centrally located high school. Elementary students continued to walk to their local schools. Today the town contracts with companies to provide regular bus routes and times for all students.

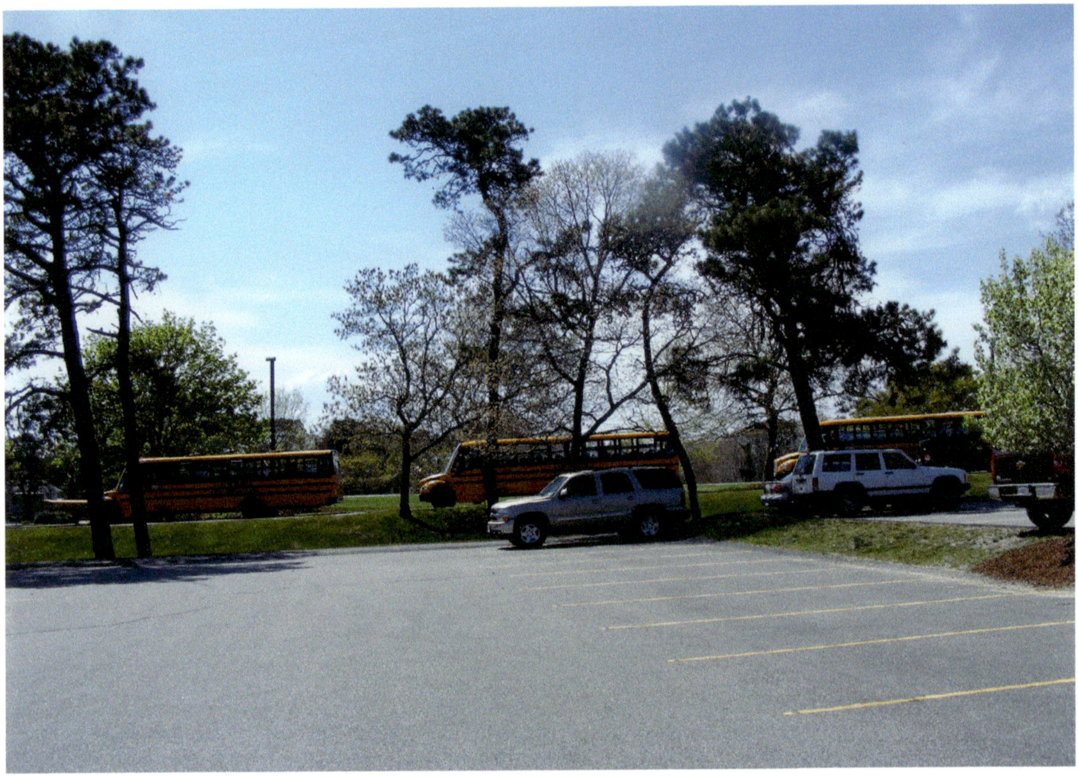

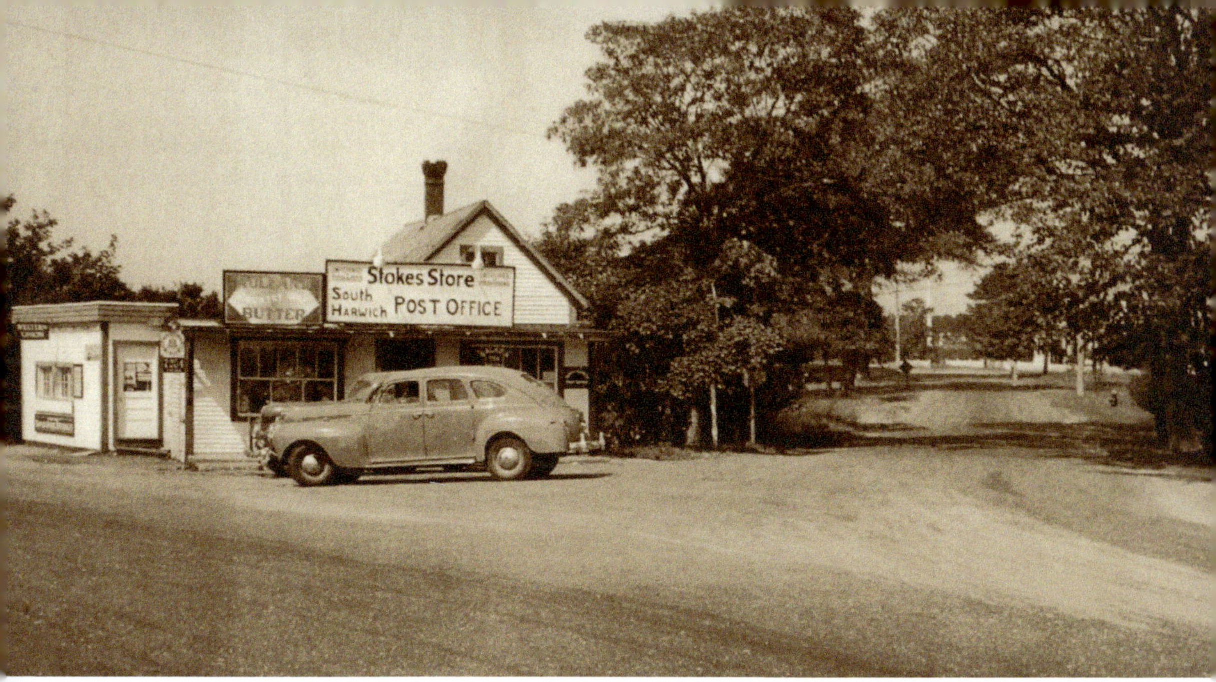

GAS STATIONS: Increasing numbers of cars and trucks created great demand for service stations. The old Stokes Store in South Harwich (which included the post office) had an ideal location for adding auto services, since it straddled the intersection of Route 28 and Chatham Road. It is now Dave's Garage, offering a variety of services including that of a locksmith.

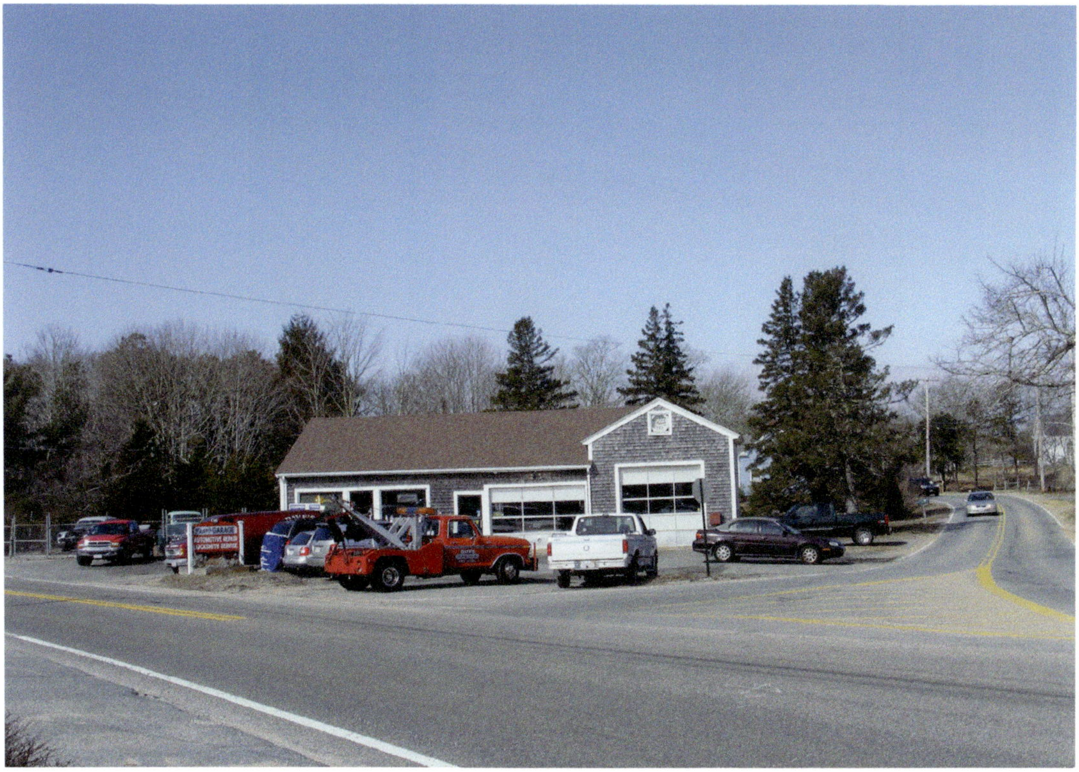

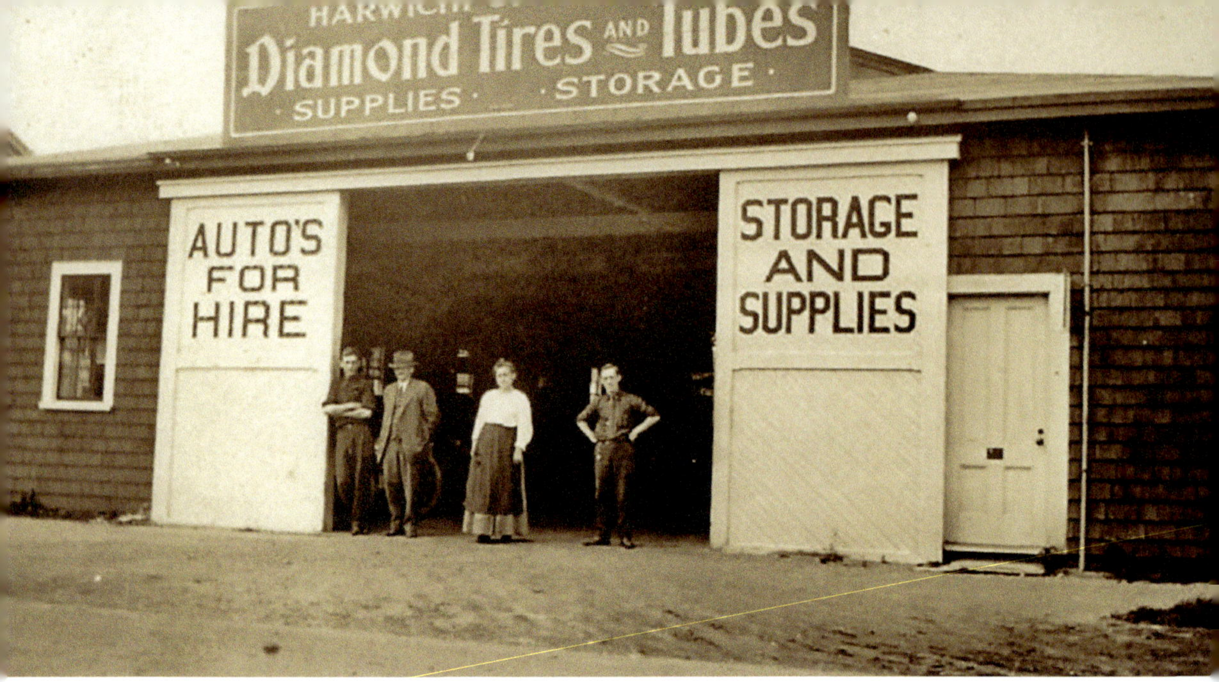

REPAIRS AND ROAD SERVICE: Ellis' Garage centrally located in Harwich Port took pride in being selected by Packard & Chrysler as their authorized agents locally. Ellis also increased his clientele by offering emergency road service whenever needed. Today the facility is the Getty station.

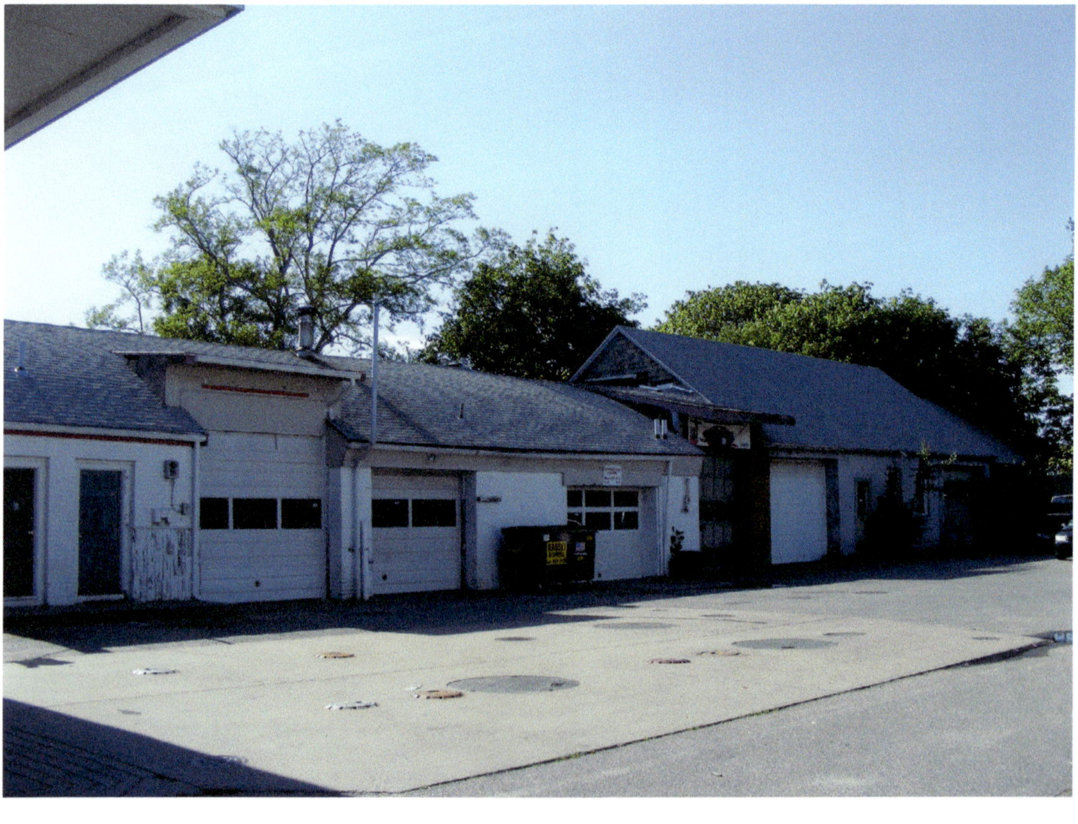

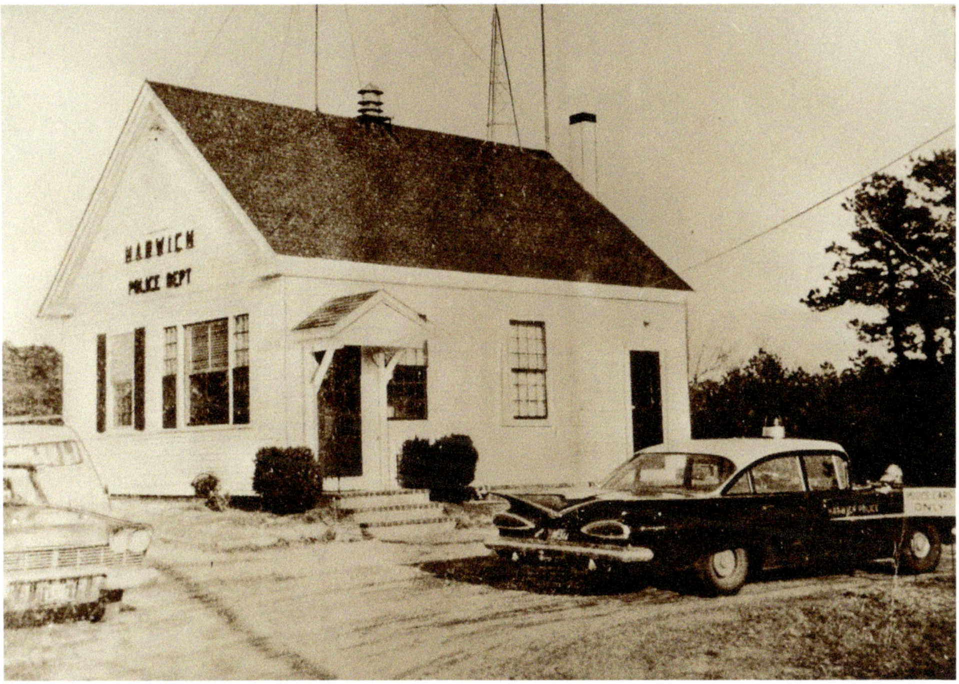

POLICING TRAFFIC: Other permanent consequences of the automobile age were the need to construct adequate roads and regulate traffic. Harwich had no full-time police force until 1930. The annual pittance for 'suppression of crim' had seldom been expended. In 1945, voters agreed to acquire several cruisers after thirty-seven accidents were reported and traffic had become 'very heavy'. The new police station on Sisson Road today is state of the art.

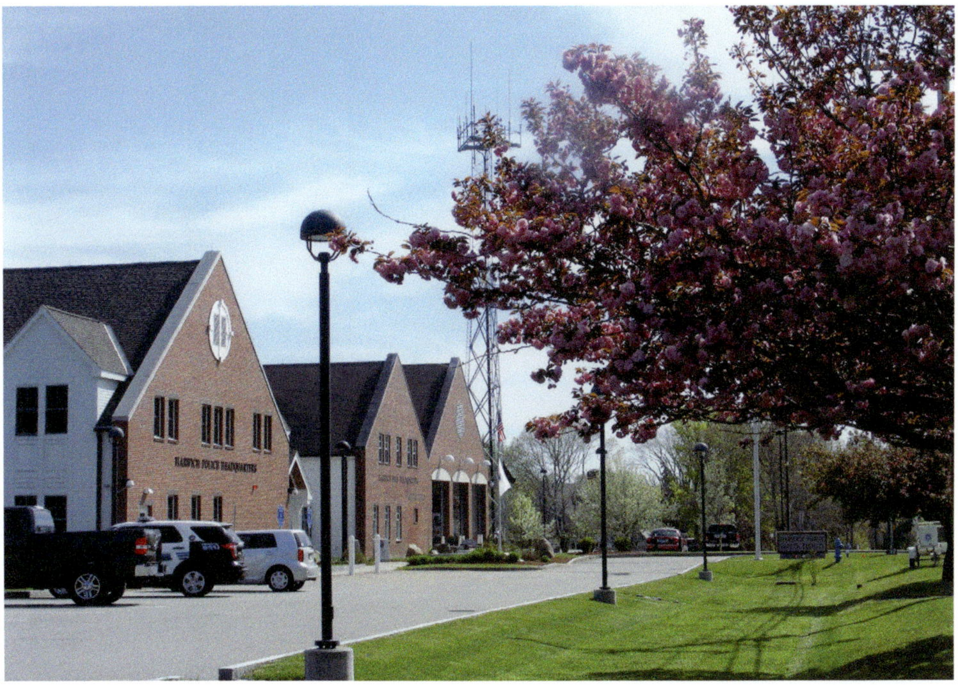

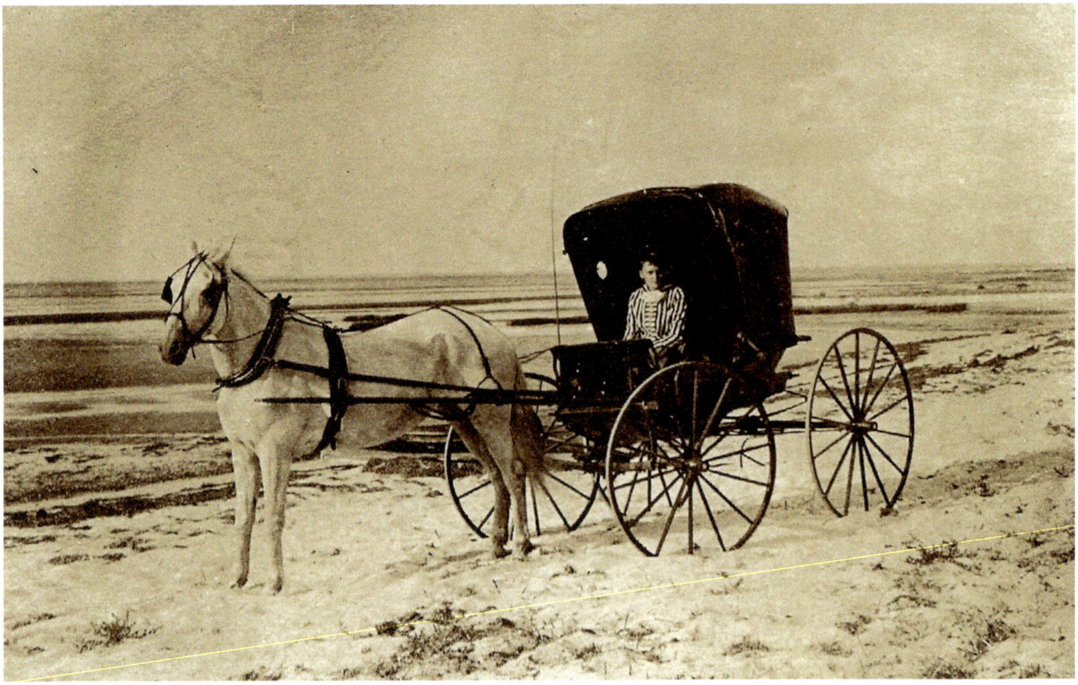

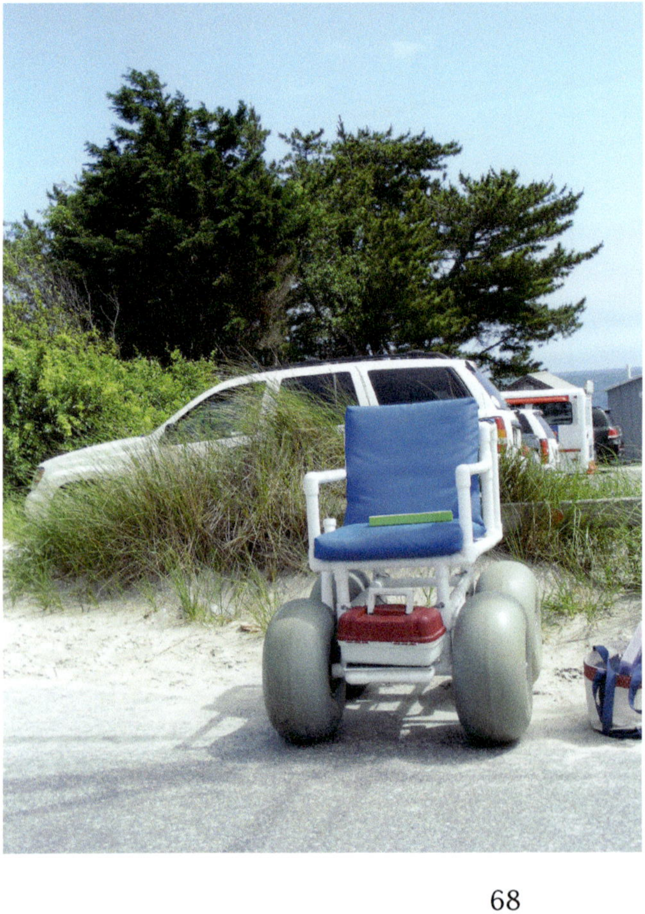

BEACH BUGGIES: A lady would no longer dare to drive her carriage by the sea: crowds of bathers often seem to cover the sand. In recent years the town has equipped several popular beaches with a new kind of 'buggy' to assist the physically challenged into the water.

BATHING BEAUTIES: A First World War era bathing beauty, outside her lodging, ponders an ocean dip. Modesty requires that she be well covered. Today a young bathing beauty has the freedom to enjoy sea and sand in a bikini. Common to both scenes is the presence of male admirers.

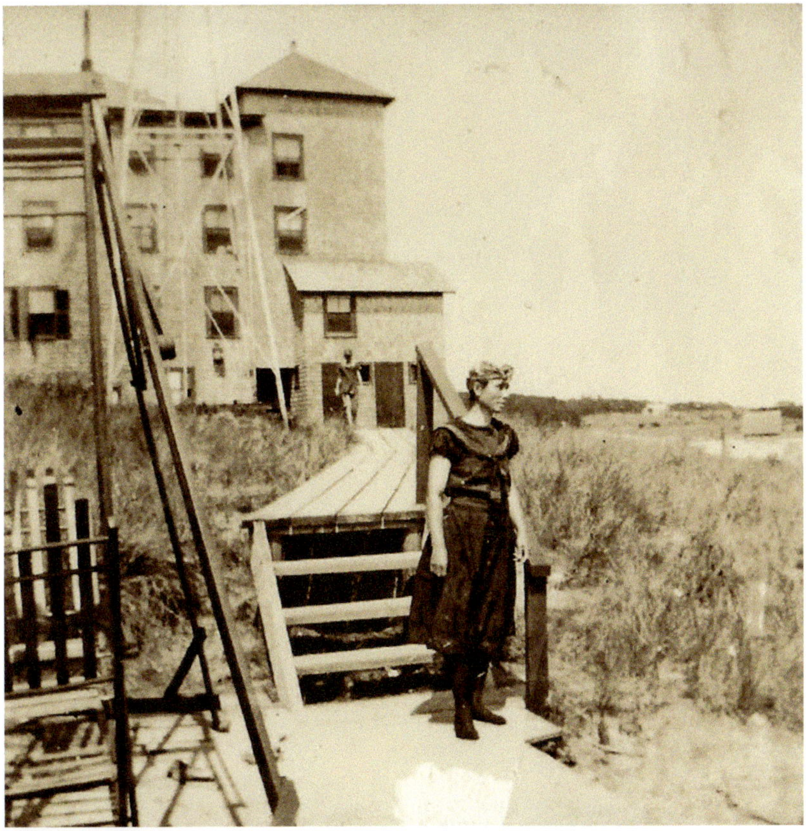

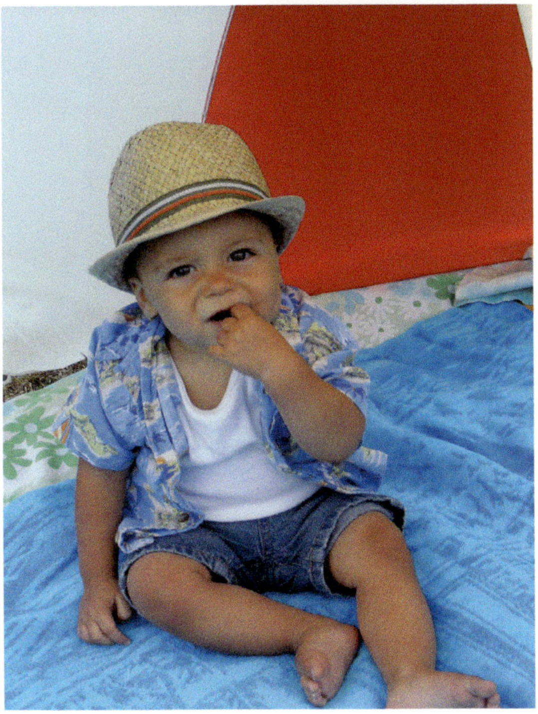

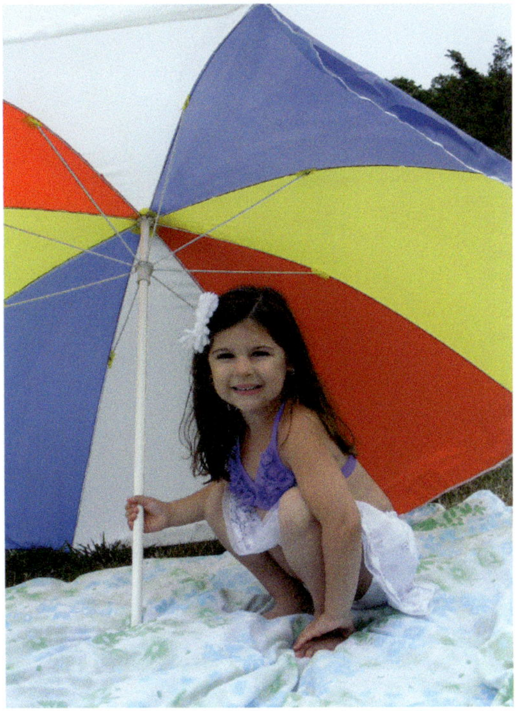

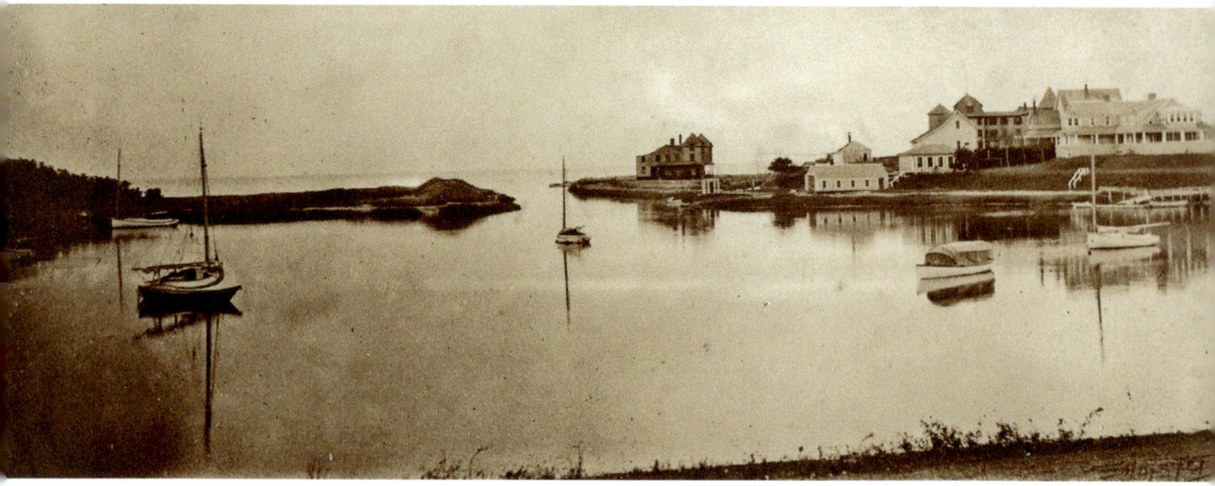

Pleasure Boats: The scenic beauty of Wychmere Harbor continues to attract admirers. The few sailboats that earlier moored there, however, have been replaced by a 'fleet' of pleasure craft and long waiting lists to obtain a mooring permit.

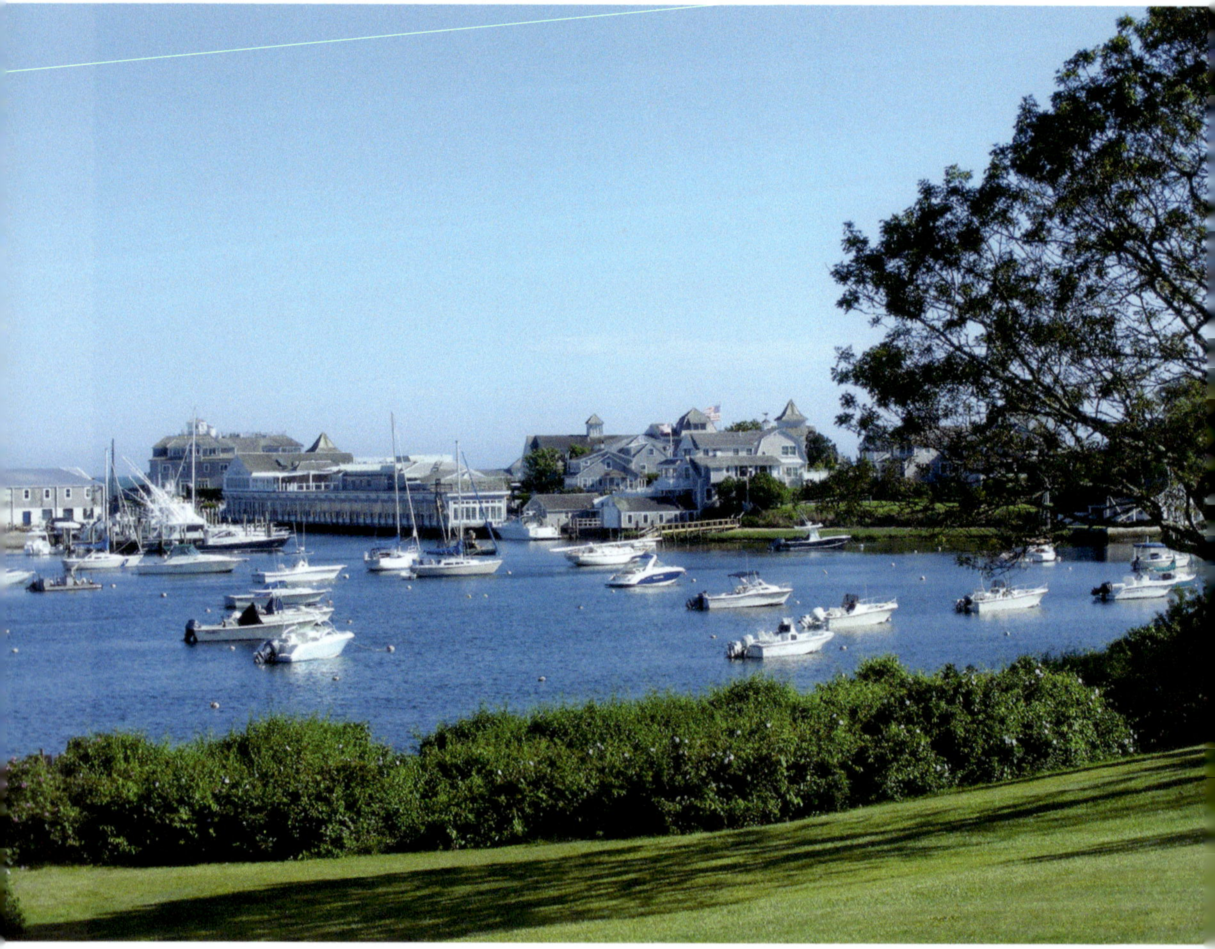

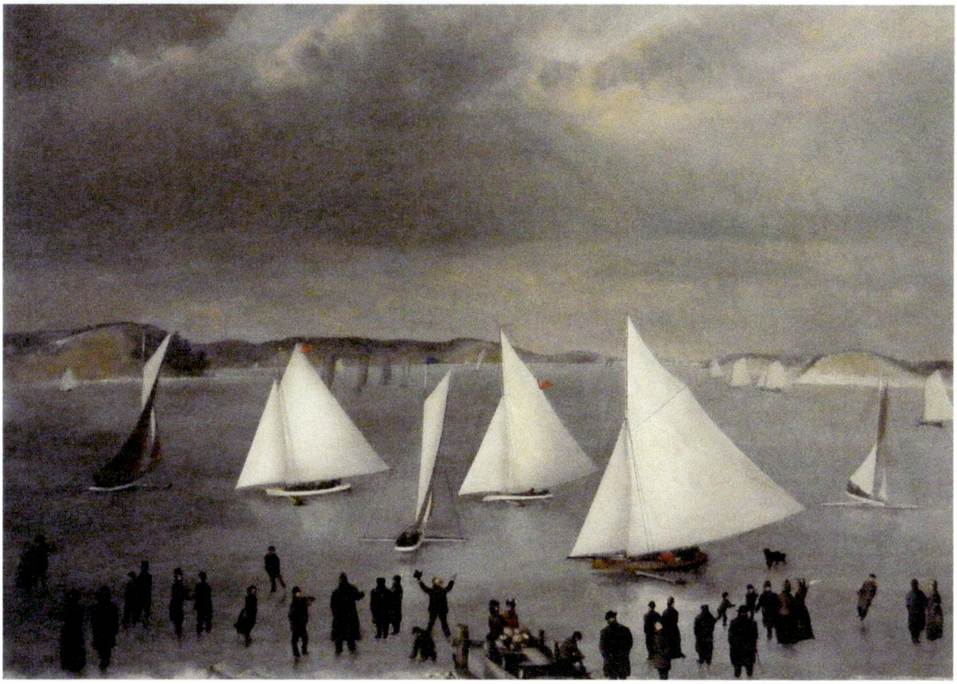

FRESH WATER PONDS: Visitors and residents alike enjoy the peacefulness and beauty of Harwich's fresh water ponds. In the late nineteenth century special trains brought winter visitors to enjoy ice-boating on Long Pond. Now kayaks are the favored craft to explore the ponds.

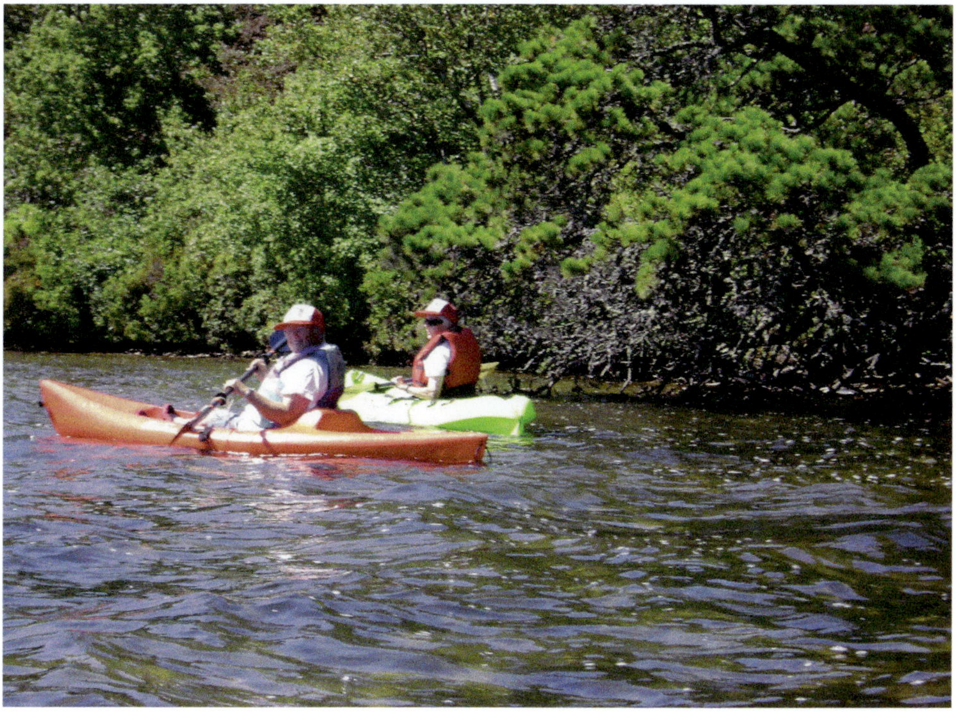

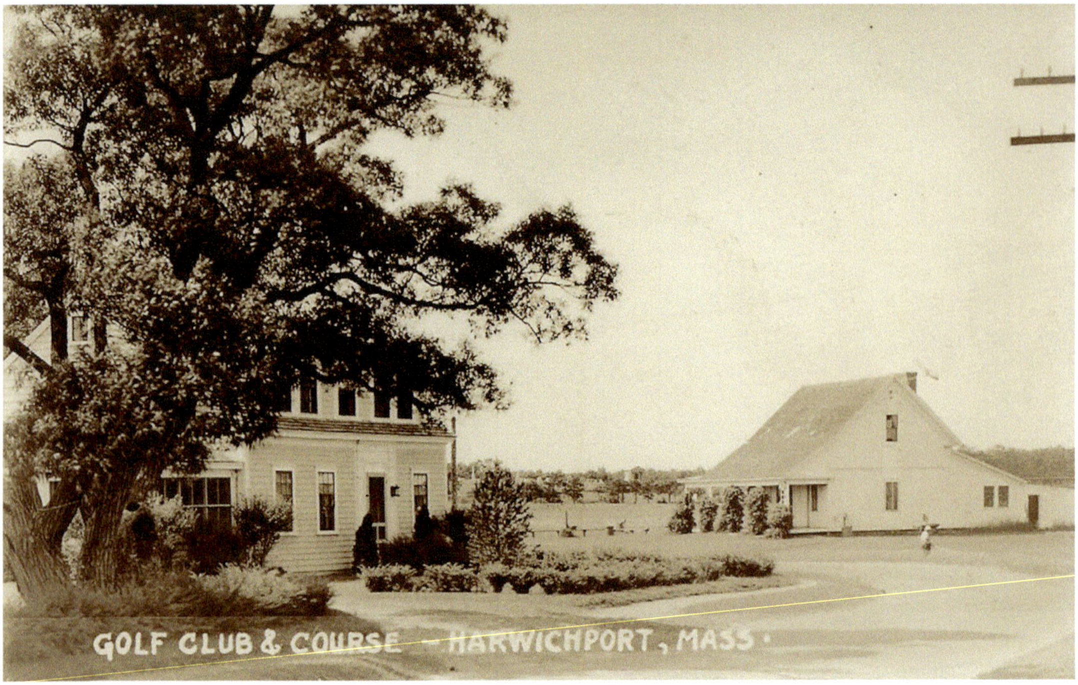

GOLFING: The Harwich Port Golf Club welcomes residents and the general public to this carefully maintained nine hole course. Few changes have been made in the facility over the years.

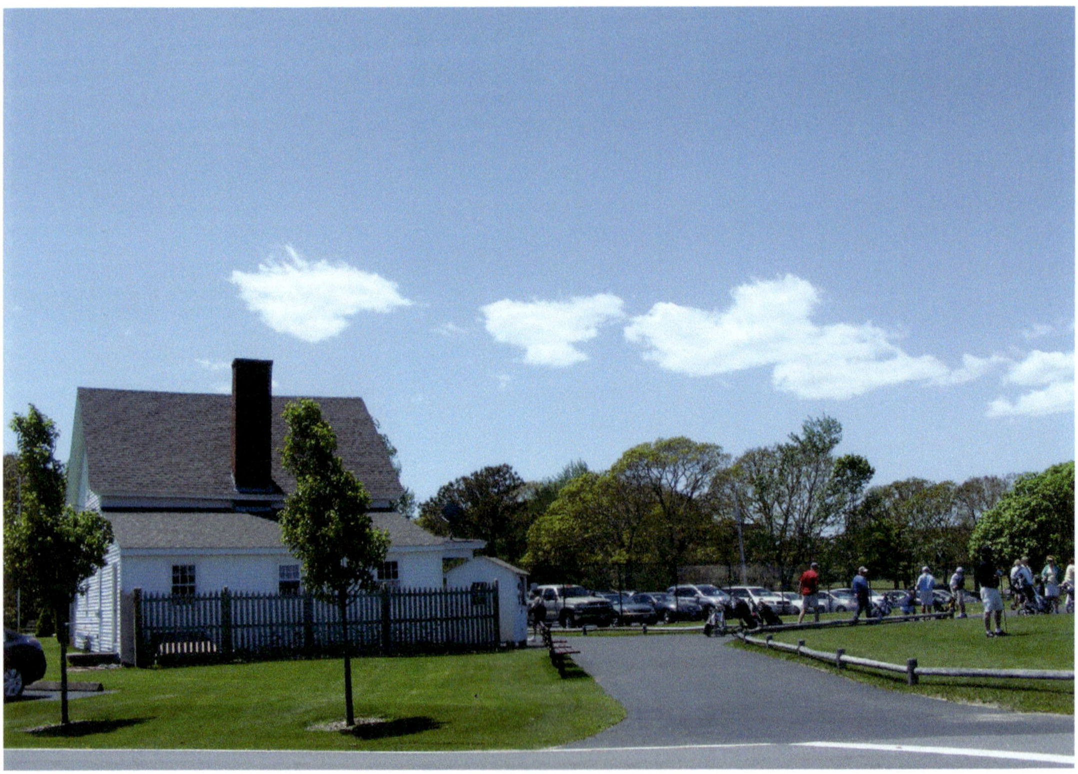

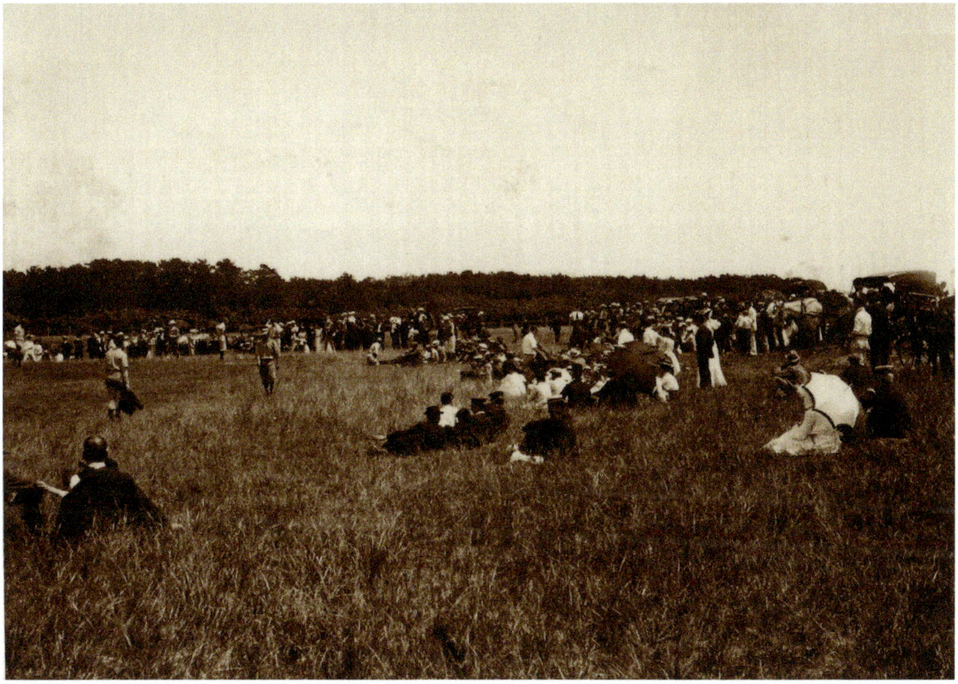

BASEBALL: Since 1900, baseball has been a popular spectator pastime in Harwich. Fans originally lounged in the deep grass to cheer their team and players barehanded balls. Today fans crowd Whitehouse Field, next to the high school, to cheer for the Harwich Mariners. The team is a member of the outstanding Cape Cod Baseball League and has sent players on to the Major Leagues.

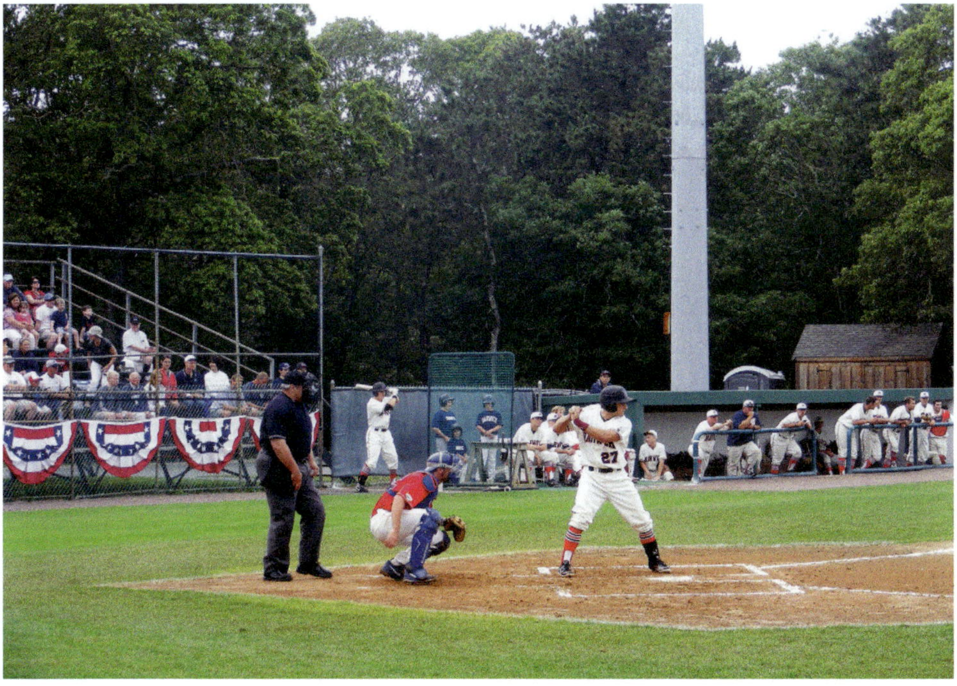

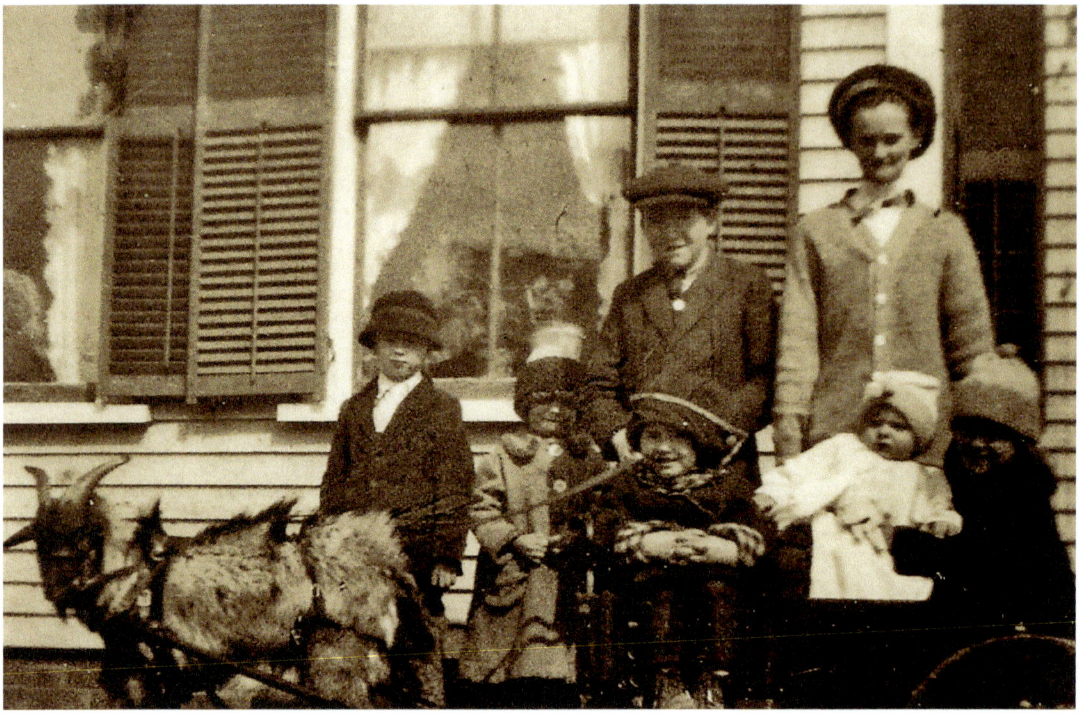

GOAT CART AND GO-CARTS: A boy's dearest wish comes true in 1907. Five-year-old Louis Dean was given his own goat and cart for his birthday. A hundred years later, in the summer season children are captivated by driving the go-carts at Bud's in Harwich Port.

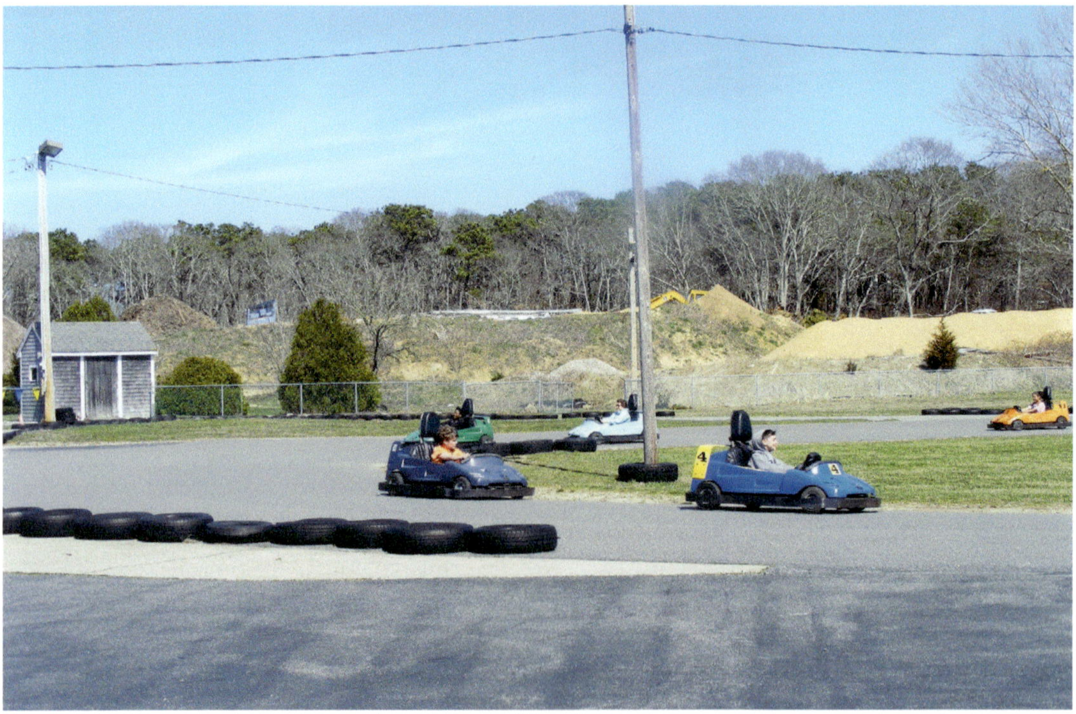

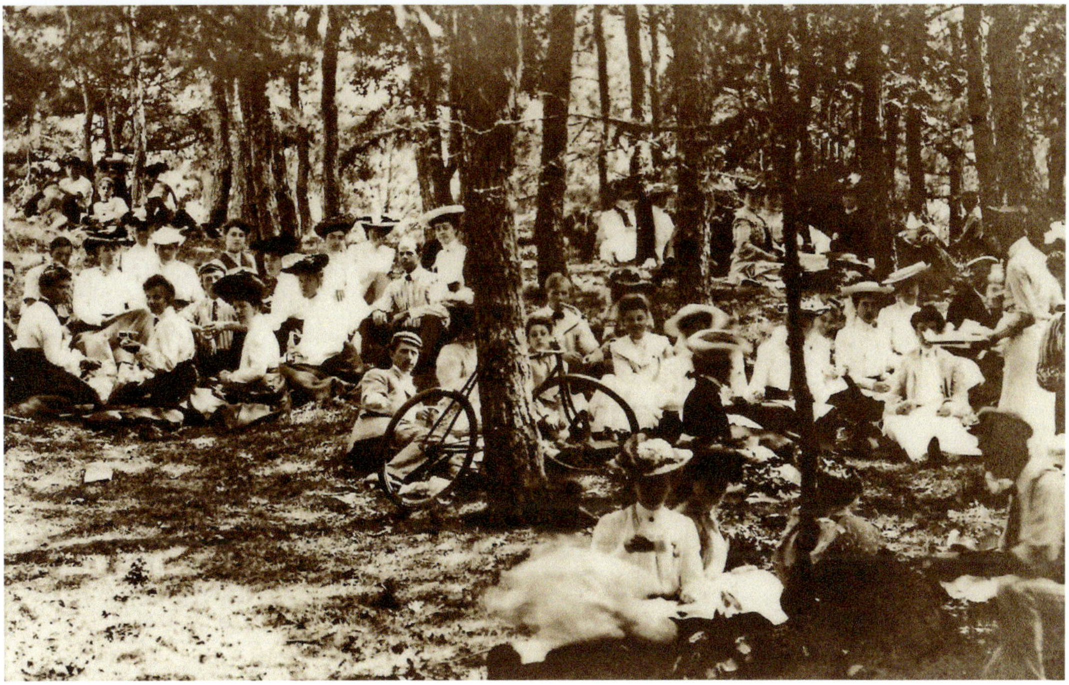

TOWN PARKS: Nothing beats picnics in the park. Brooks Grove, now called Brooks Park, has been a favored picnic spot since Victorian times. Ladies sipped tea served by attentive beaus. Today, in addition to picnic areas, this park offers ball fields, tennis courts, and a charming bandstand for summer concerts.

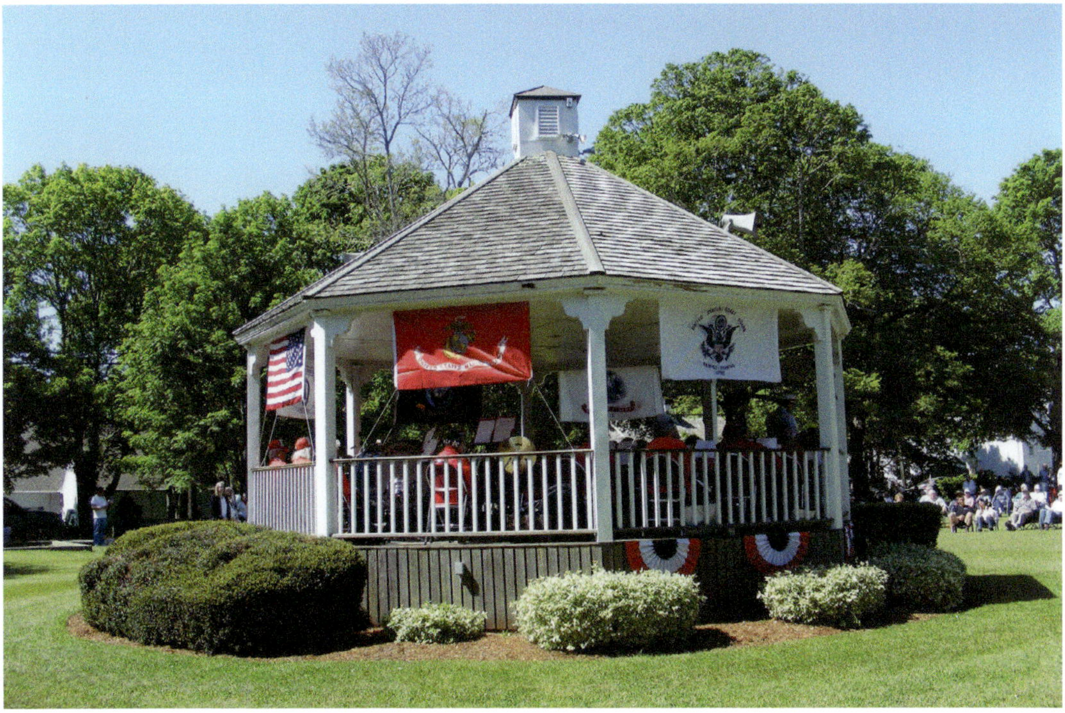

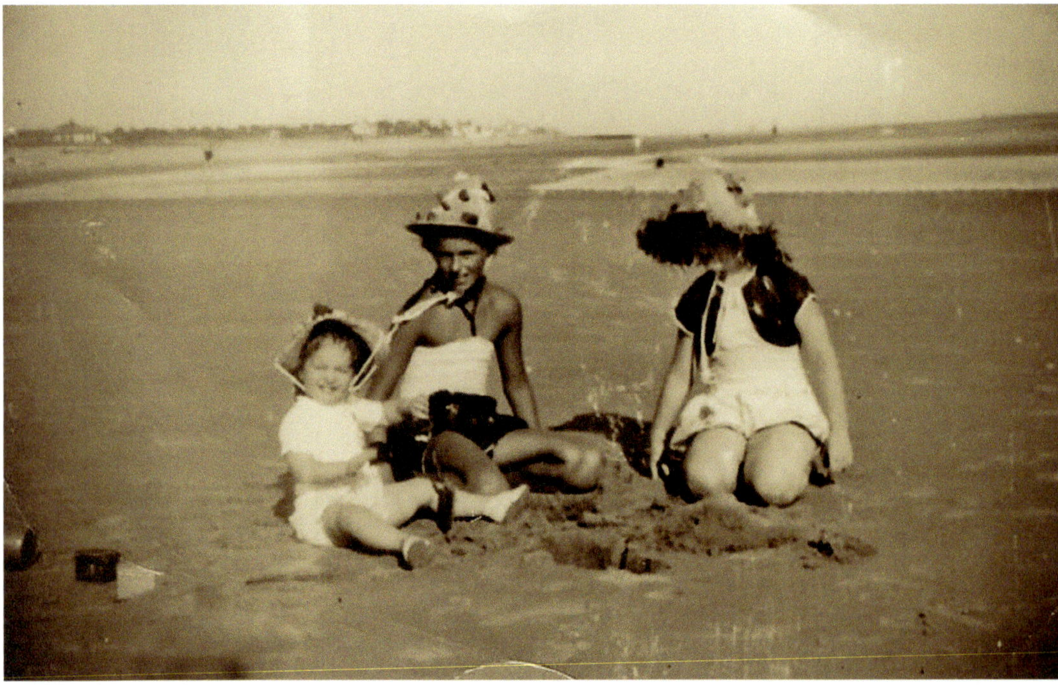

SAND CASTLES: A child's joy in building sand castles or splashing in the ocean's waters seems timeless. In the 1950s, three girls plan their castle. In the second photograph, the children protect their work from marauding seagulls.

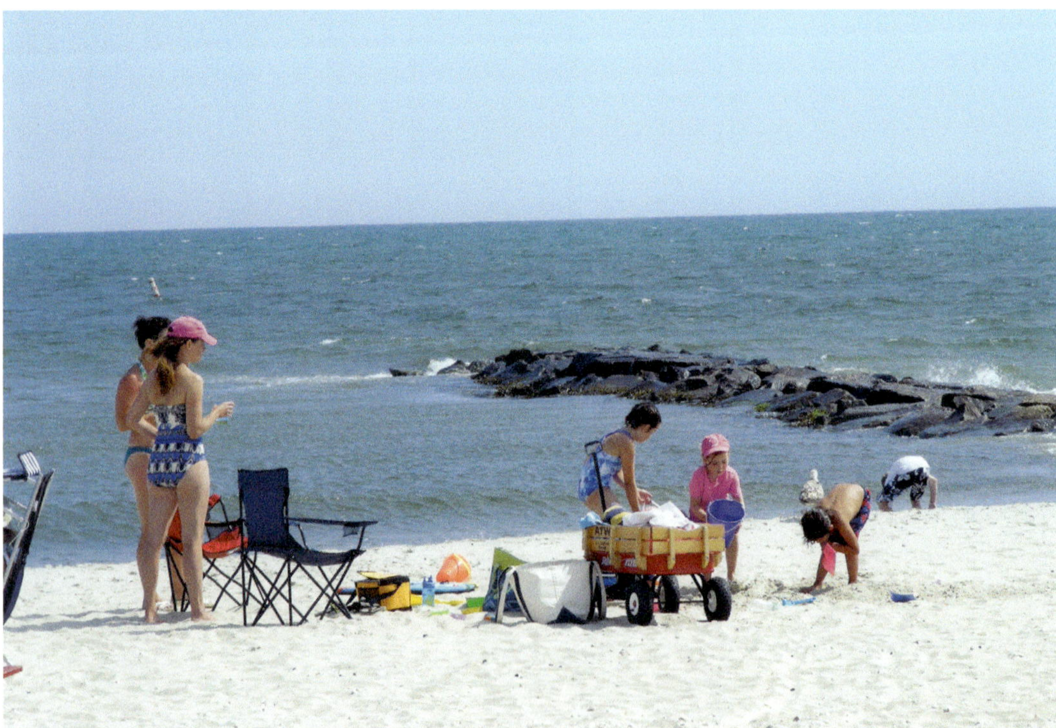

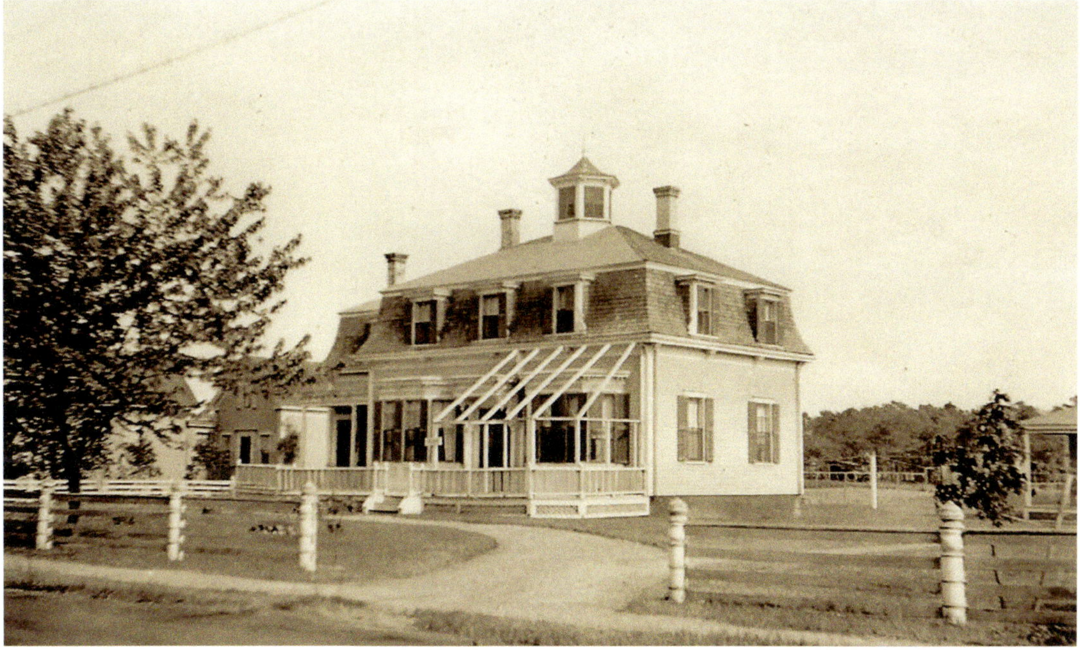

LODGINGS: The influx of summer visitors demanded an expansion of housing facilities. Some older buildings were modified: the Melrose in Harwich Port is a fine example. Located only a block from the beach, it was originally a small, seasonal inn. It became a popular year round hotel, and is now a thriving condominium.

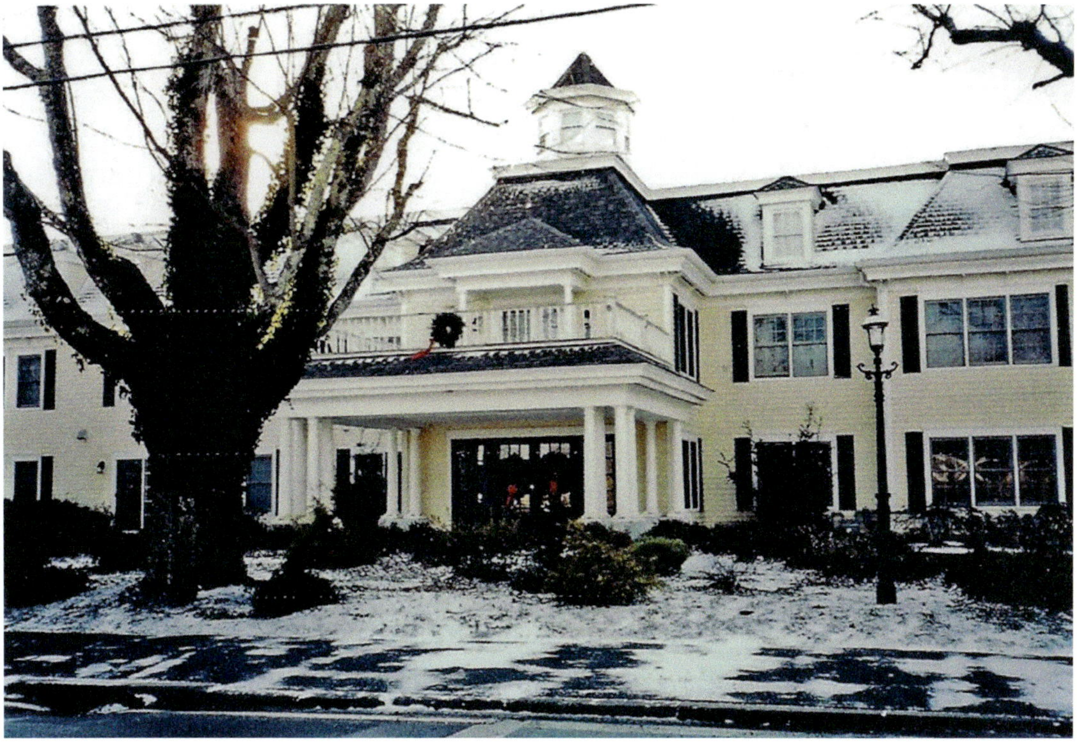

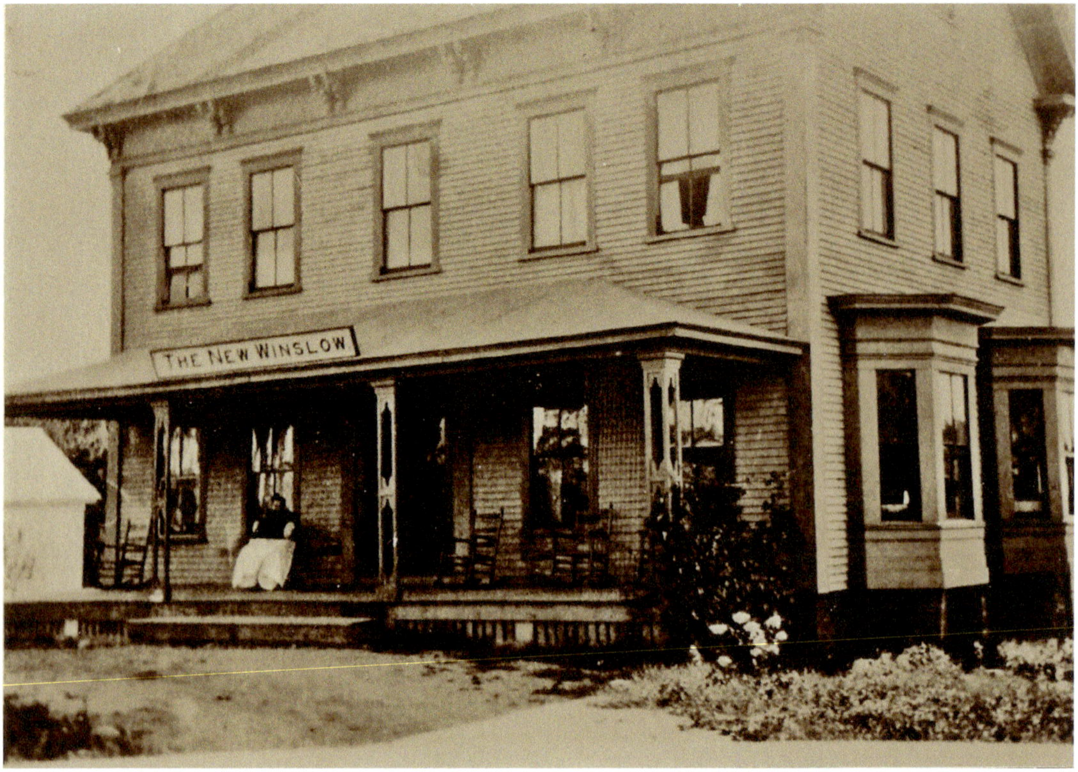

SPECIAL FACILITIES: Another old building took a different course. The Hotel Winslow was built in Harwich Center, and rebuilt on Bank Street after the first structure was destroyed by fire. The Winslow eventually seemed destined to die of neglect, until the Winsteads restored it with expanded amenities. More recently, it has begun a new chapter as the Royal, a homelike assisted-living facility.

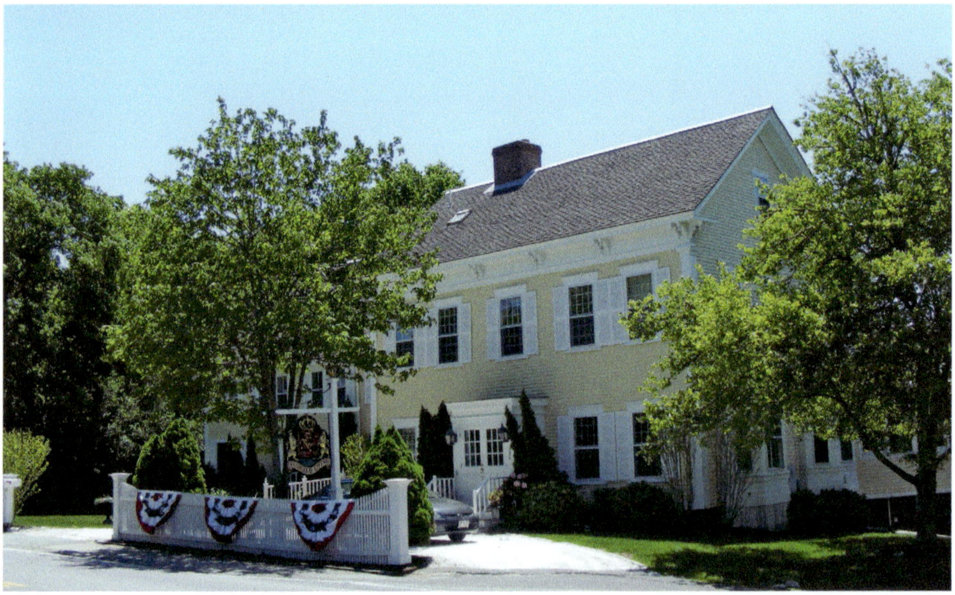

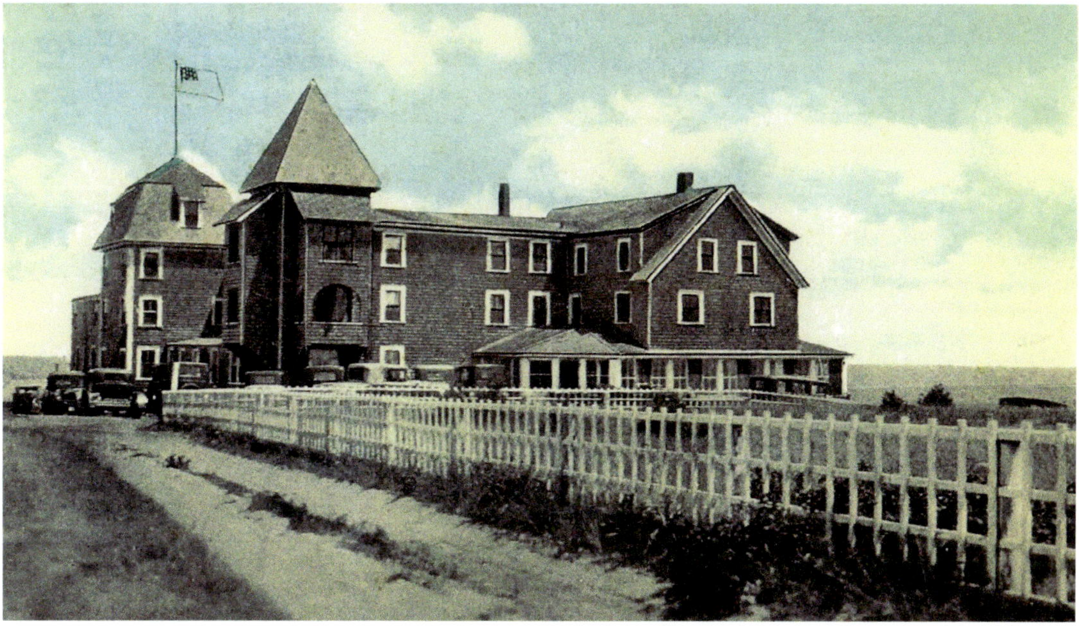

BEACHFRONT COMPLEXES: The Snow Inn began taking in paying guests in 1892, after the owner of a small, beachfront cottage added twenty rooms to stop free visiting by relatives. The condominium complex now includes fourteen acres of prime waterfront on Nantucket Sound, including a private beach, tennis courts and restaurants.

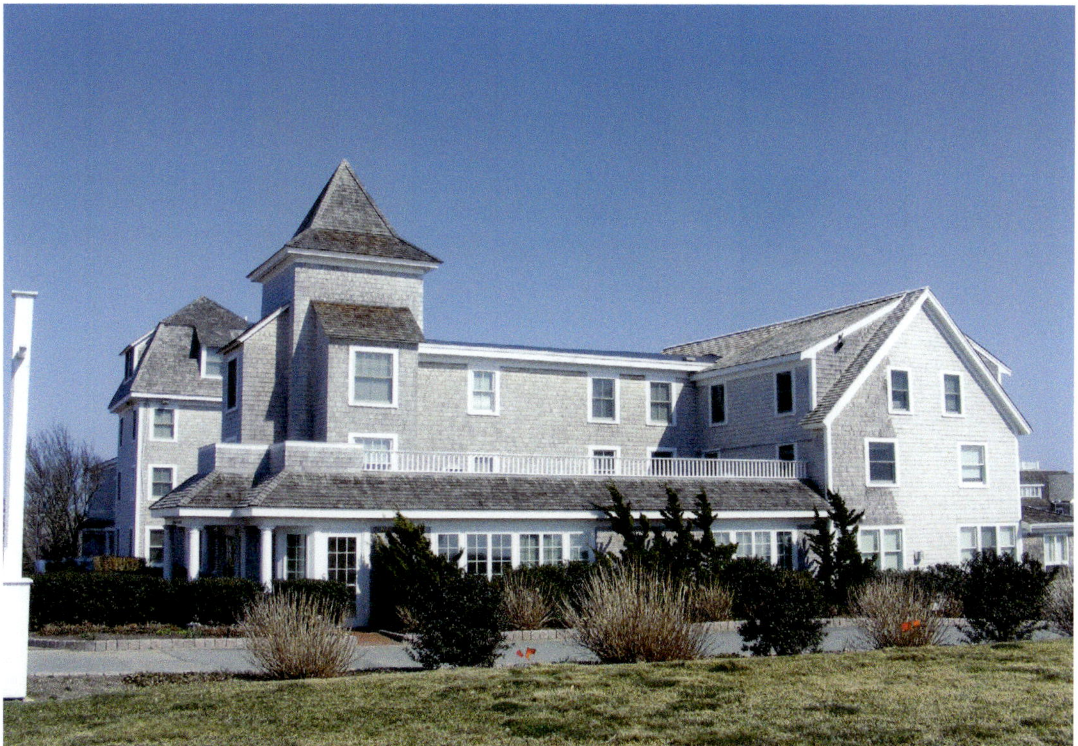

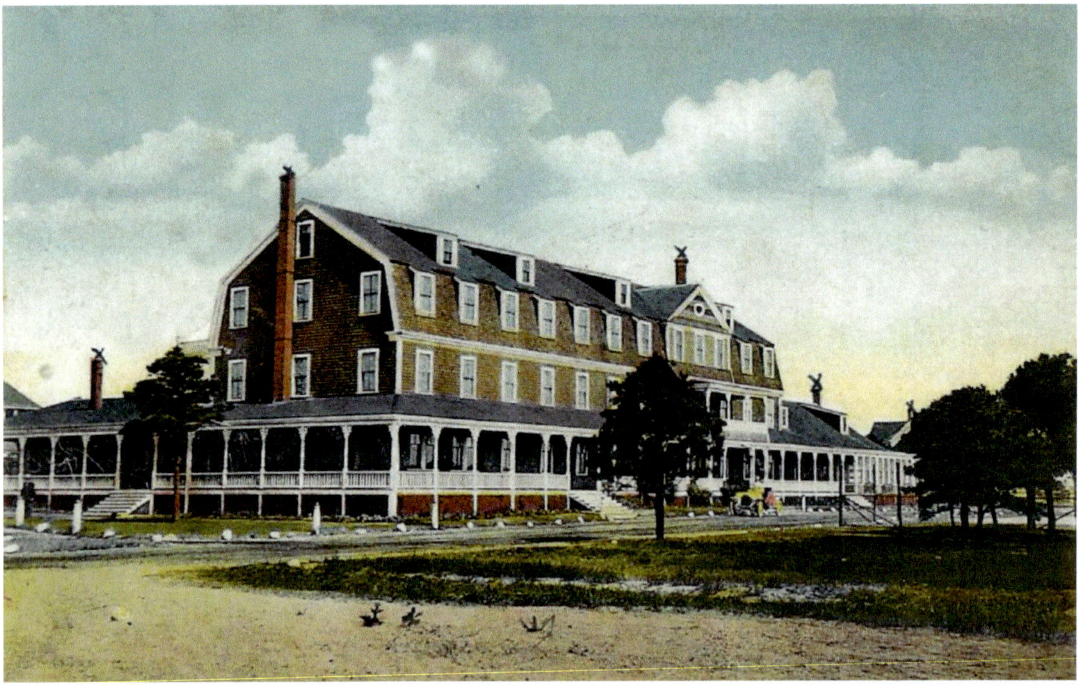

THE FIRST GRAND HOTEL: The Belmont was erected in West Harwich in 1893 as a premier hotel, for a clientele often arriving by railroad to enjoy its twenty-two acres, including a private beach, and various special services. The hotel was often referred to as the 'Summer Wall Street', since it installed the first Dow Jones ticker for use of its many New York guests. The old hotel was razed; a large condominium complex replaces it.

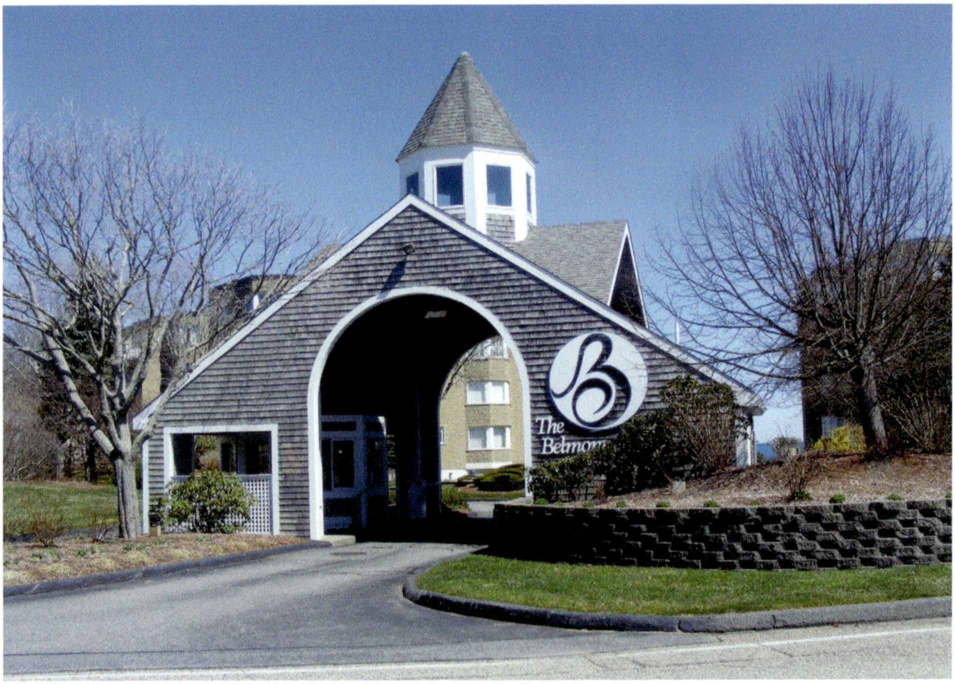

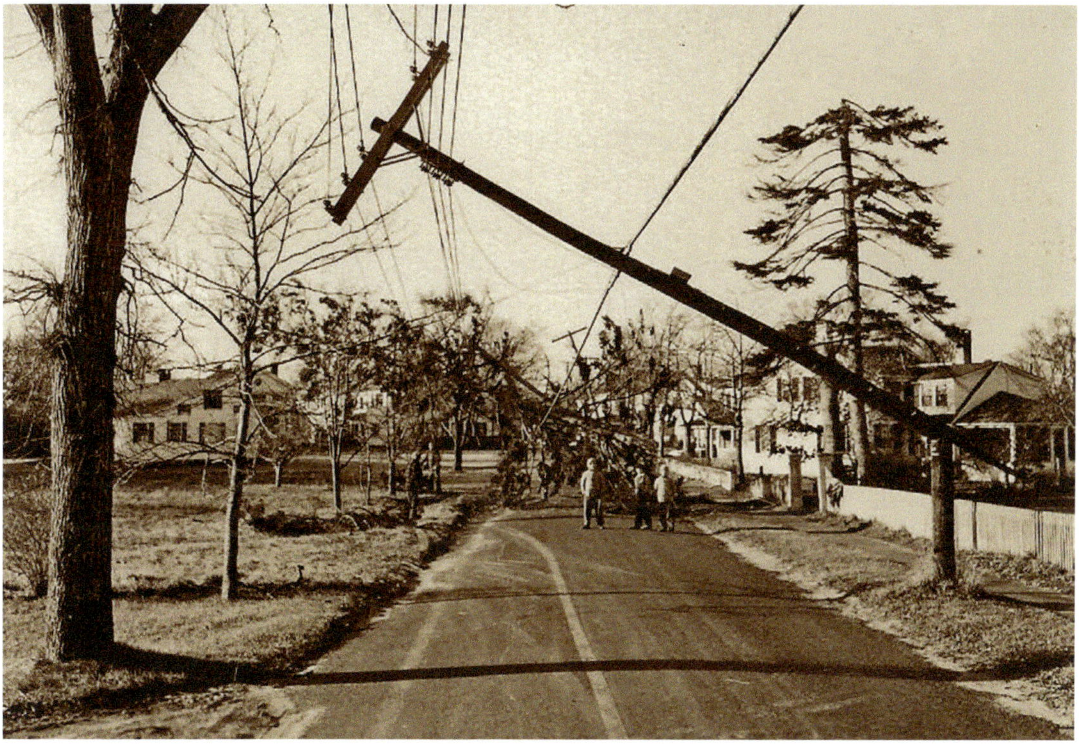

NATURAL DISASTERS: The labor to preserve and protect town treasures of aging buildings and the town's natural resources is endless. Cape Cod is a slender peninsula jutting out into the North Atlantic and storms are a constant concern. The worst destruction comes from hurricanes and nor'easters. The downed power lines on Bank Street during the 1944 storm and the toppled trees and outhouse of 1991's Hurricane Bob are but small samples of the threat.

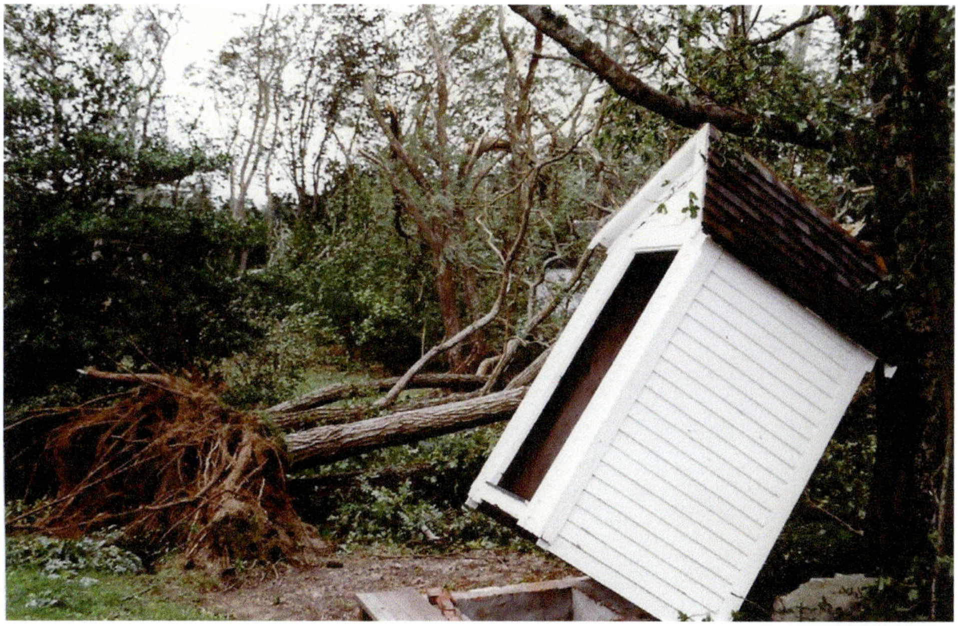

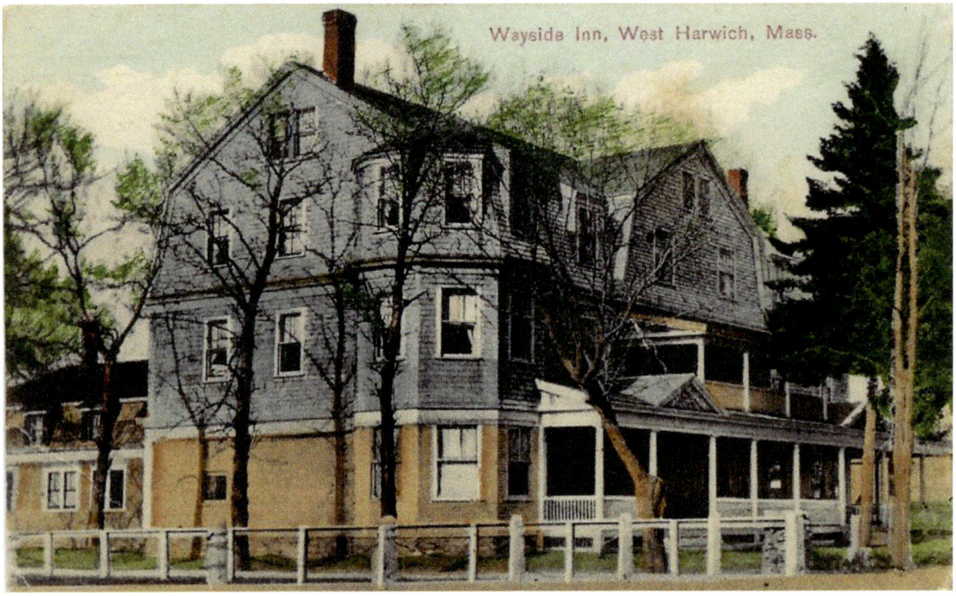

FIRE LOSSES: The most common danger over the years comes from fire, including those earlier caused by sparks flying from passing trains. The attempt to douse major fires by buckets of water drawn from wells or carried from the nearest pond and passed from hand to hand rarely was effective in quelling the flames. The Wayside Inn was constructed in West Harwich by Caleb Chase in 1906. After he died, this elegantly furnished inn was leased to the Sea Pines School for Girls. In 1909 it was totally destroyed by a fire that began in a beam behind a fireplace. It is now the site of the Harwich Antiques Center.

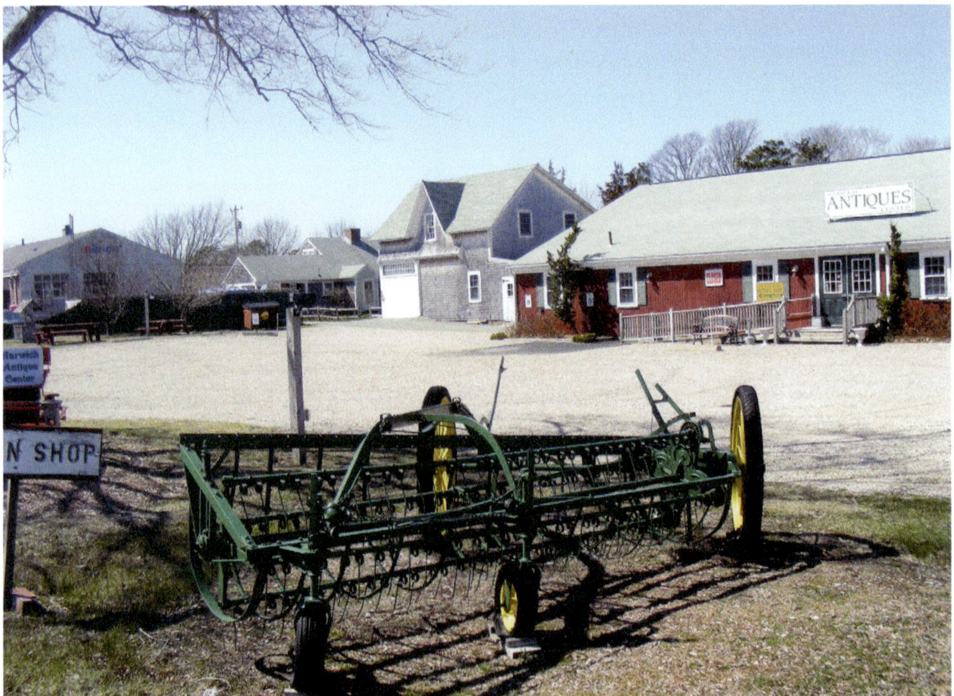

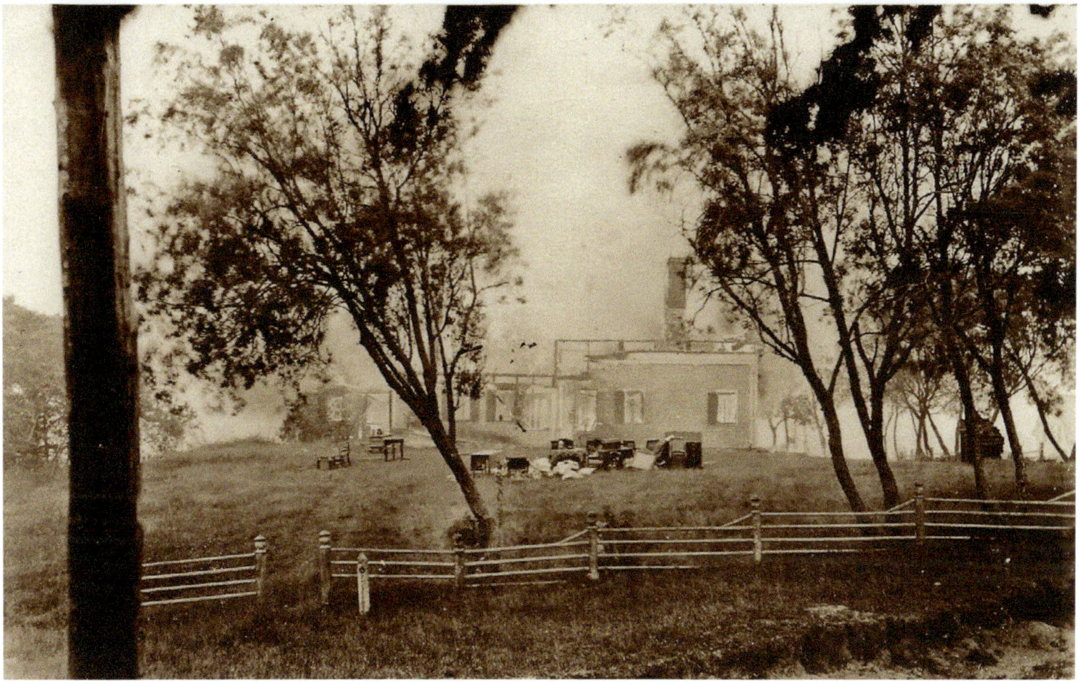

MASSIVE FIRE IN SOUTH HARWICH: A single fire in South Harwich burned 3,200 acres and destroyed thirteen dwellings before it was brought under control. But it was not until the late 1920s that voters approved purchase of a pumping engine capable of drawing water from area ponds. The former system of volunteer firemen is now replaced by a full contingent of responders to both fire and medical emergencies. Their state of the art station now adjoins the police station on Sisson Road.

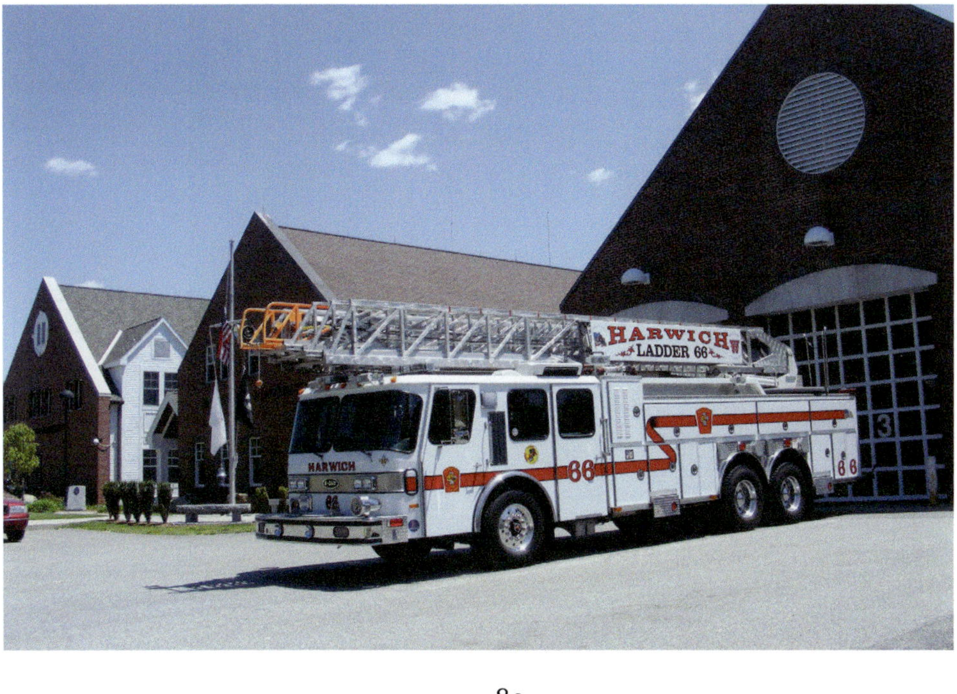

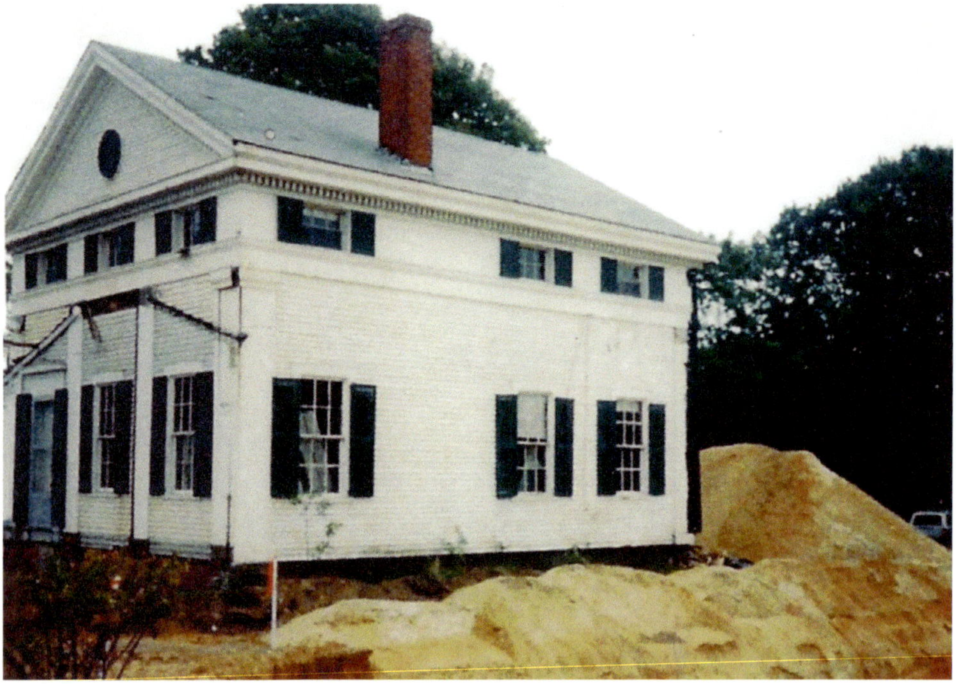

Conservation of Buildings: Sometimes old buildings can be saved by moving them to a more welcoming site. This practice was easier with old structures, since their supporting beams were on the ground rather than in dug foundations. A large structure was 'flaked' into smaller, more manageable sections. In at least one case, a home was moved with all its furnishings intact, even the chimney, with the owner sleeping in his own bed each night on the road! Some houses, however, have been damaged or neglected to the point that they must be declared uninhabitable and torn down.

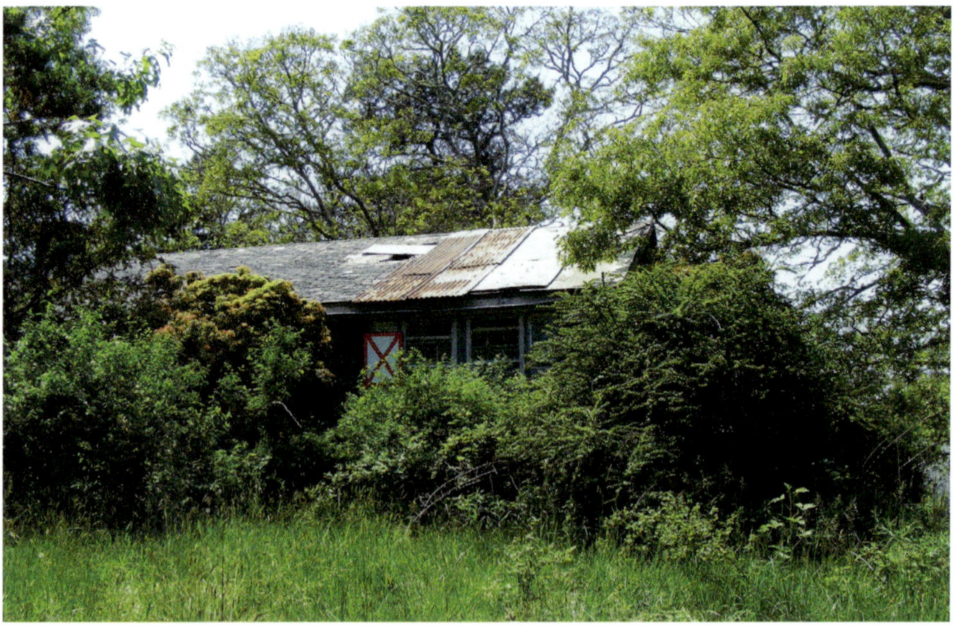

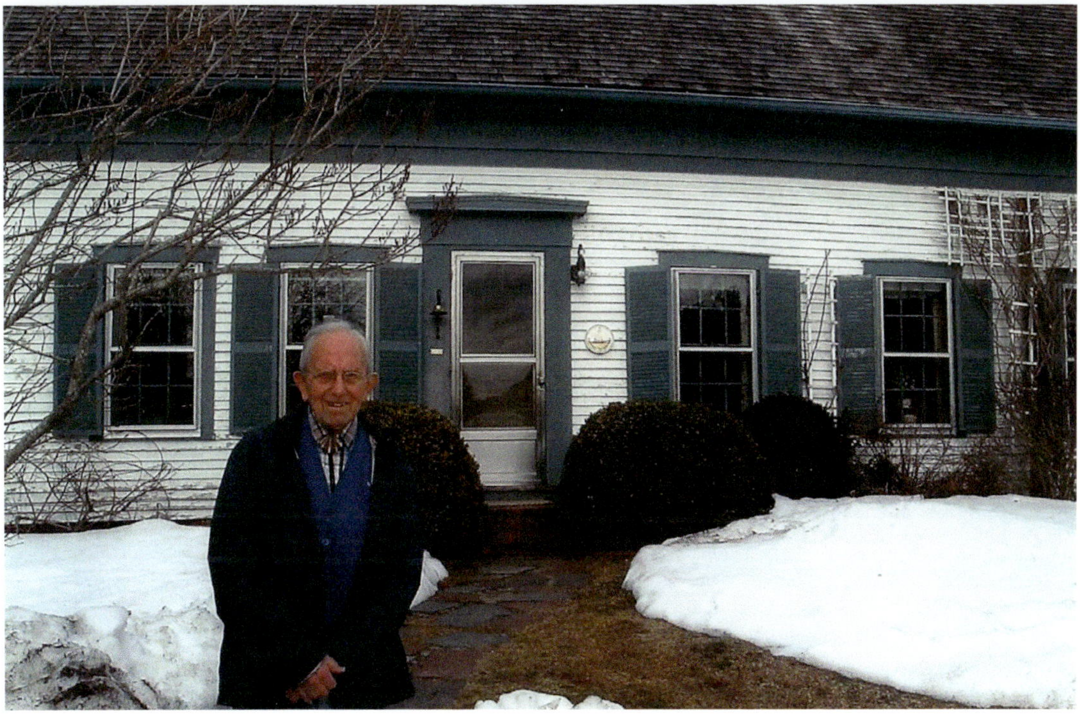

Razing for Other Reasons: Some structures are sacrificed when the land under them is deemed more valuable than the building. This beautiful old, colonial style home is an example. The house was likely built in the 1840s on seven acres of meadow. It was recently destroyed so that a western-style horse farm could use the acres.

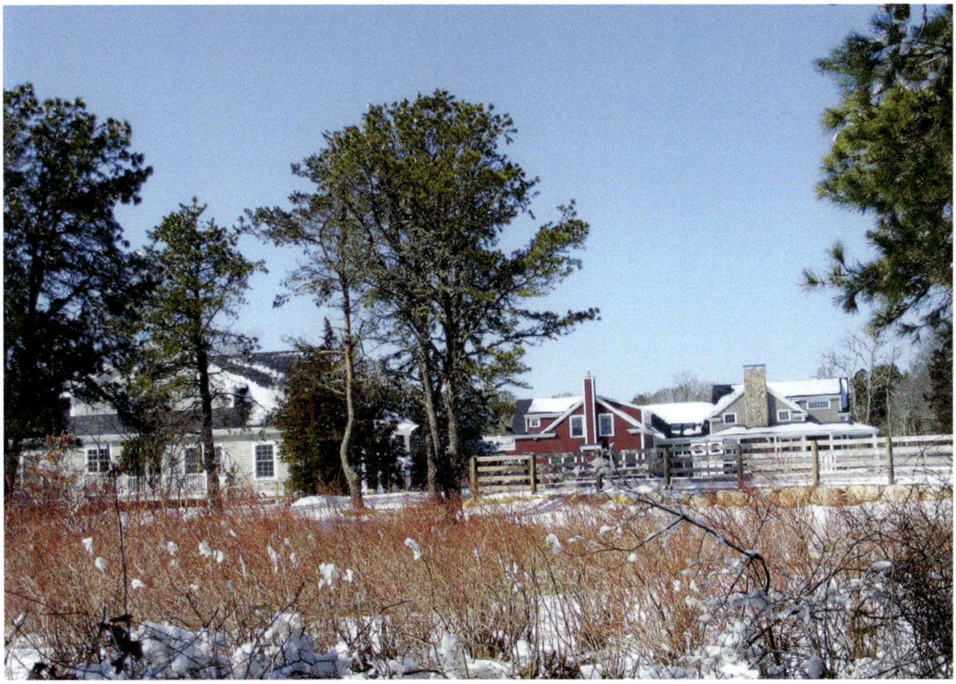

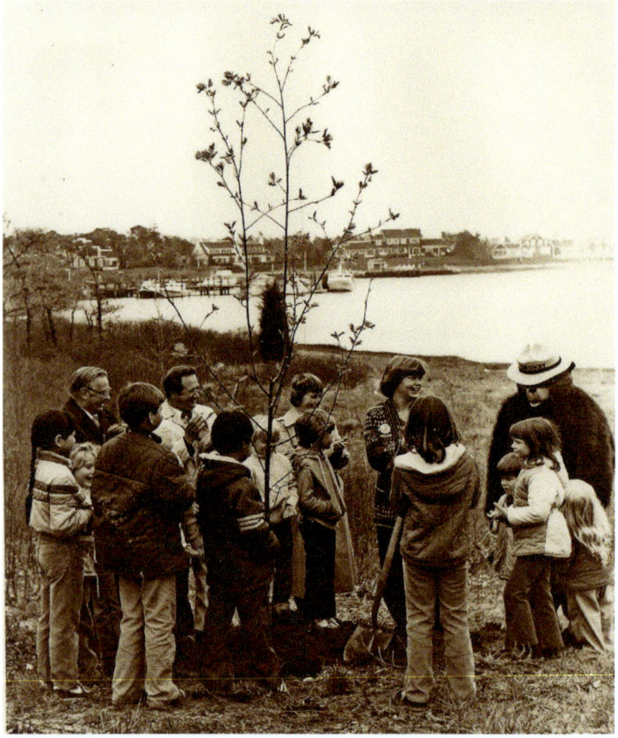

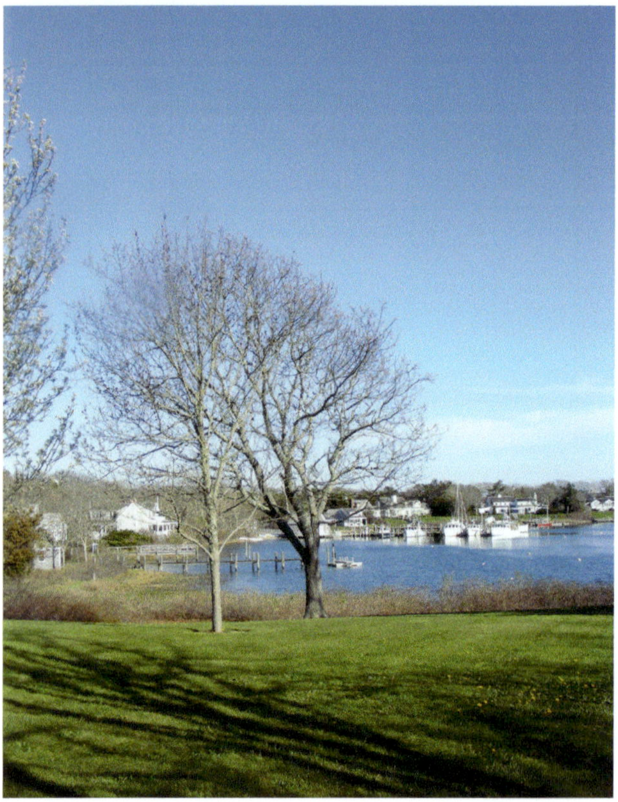

NATURAL CONSERVATION:
Smokey the Bear in 1981 encouraged children to plant trees on the northern slope of Wychmere Harbor. This site is often favored by travelers stopping to take photographs. The landscape, even to the trees, is remarkably unchanged.

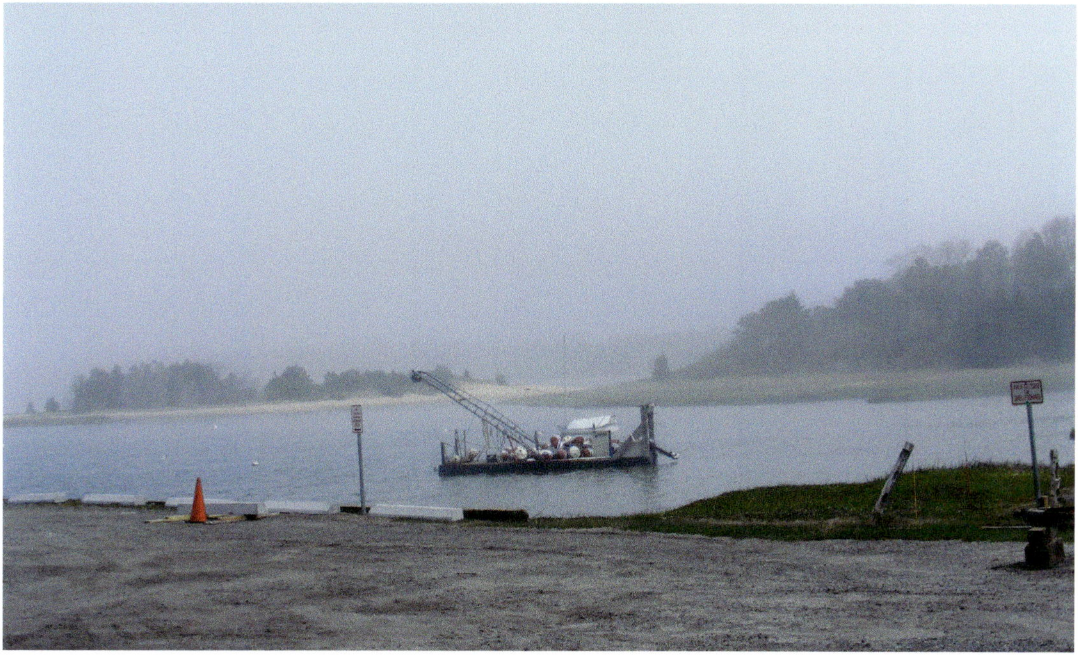

MONITORING WATERWAYS: A harbormaster's scow, in the early morning mist, checks moorings in Pleasant Bay to protect the waters. Another means of protection is the encouragement of recycling. The 'treasure chest' in the town disposal facility promotes neighbors helping neighbors by exchanging a wide variety of useable articles.

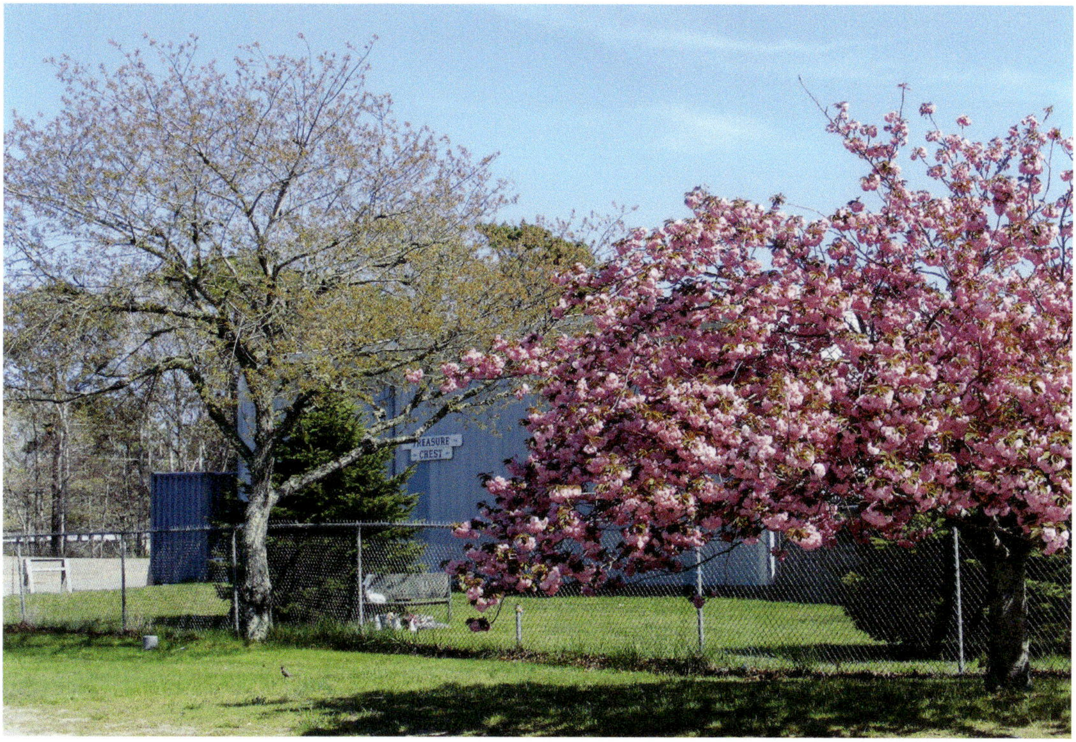

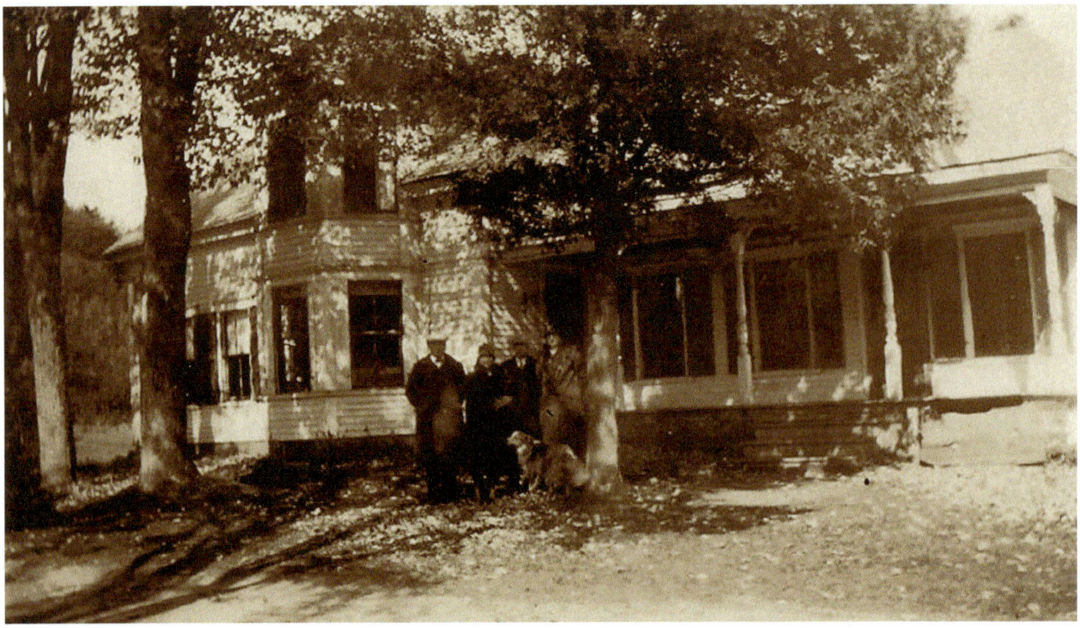

PRESERVING HOUSES: Property owners in the Center's Historic District are especially dedicated to preservation. This home is an excellent example. It was built by a shoemaker in 1844 in the shadows of the academy. The owner shrewdly added a section that could be rented to teachers and students, and ran his shoe-making business from a small outbuilding. The present owners have meticulously restored the house. The barn now provides space for weaving fine silks sold worldwide.

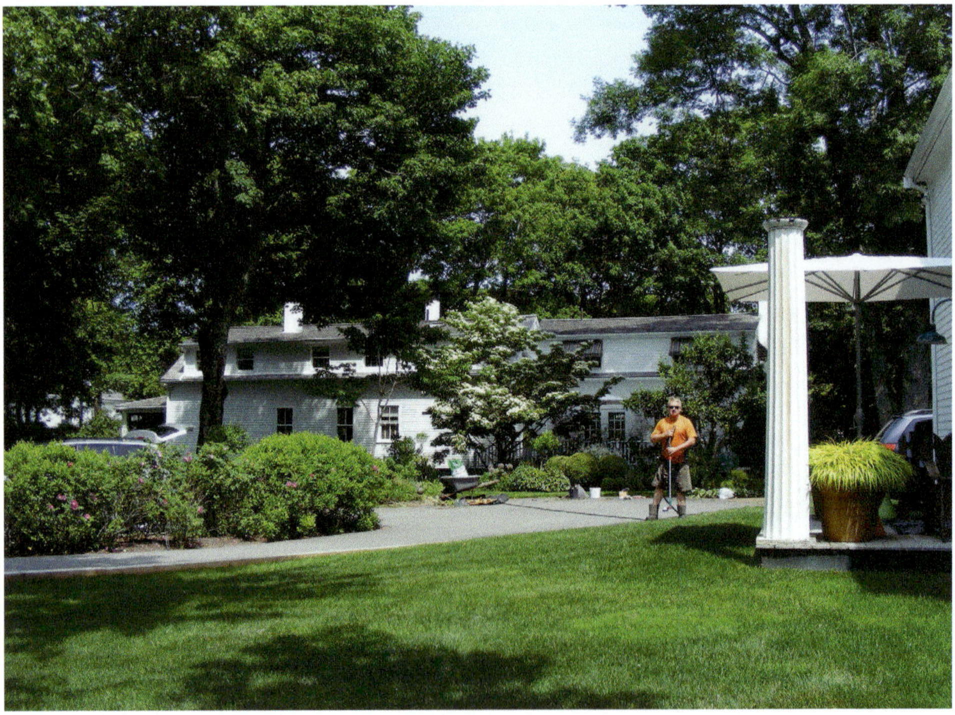

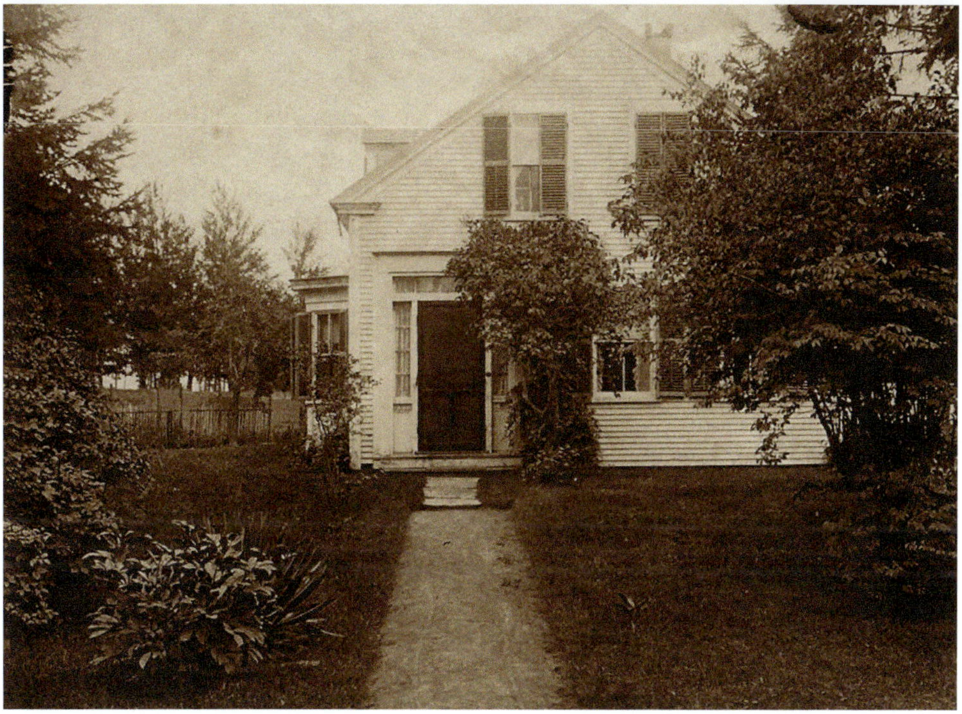

RESTORATIONS: Across from the shoemaker was the home of his eldest brother. Generations of members of the same family enjoyed this home from the early 1830s until the 1950s. The property then deteriorated, to the point where part of the roof caved in. A young and dedicated restoration expert has brought the home back to its original integrity and charm.

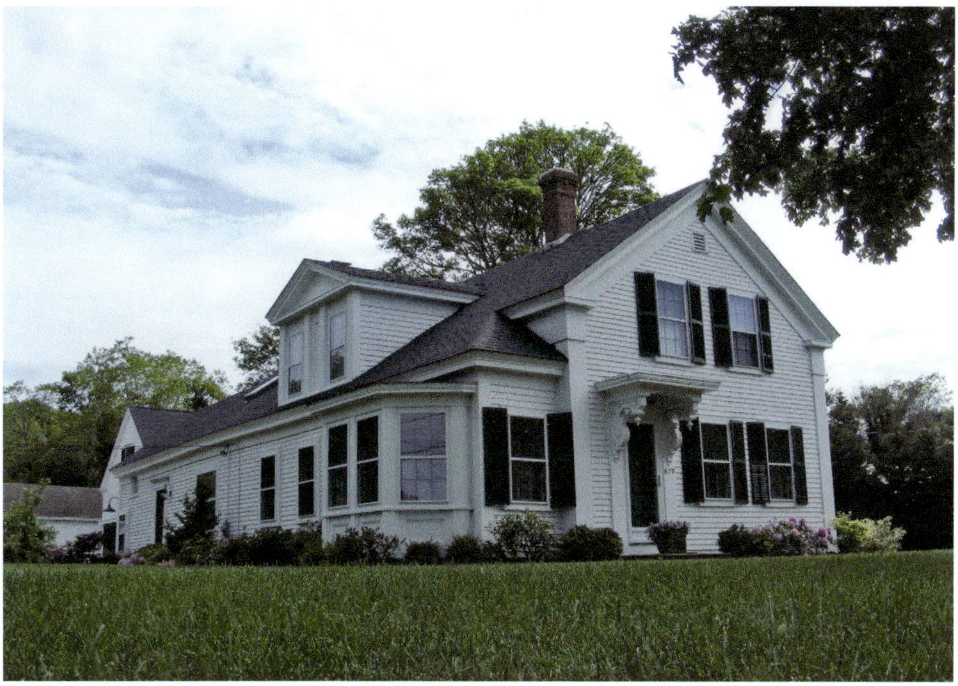

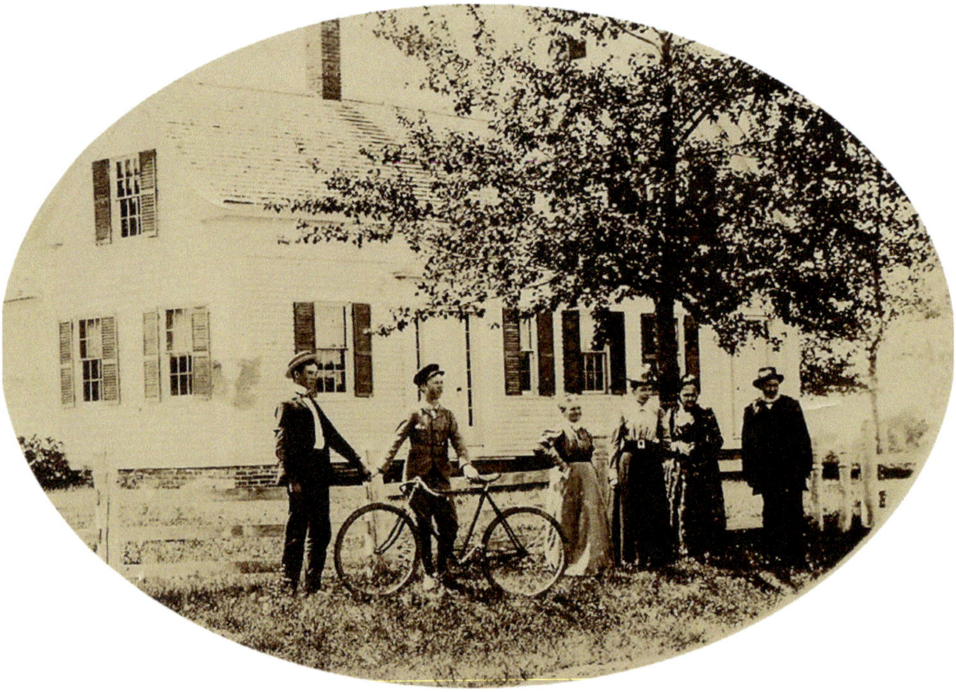

CHANGING COMMUNICATIONS: Change, most assuredly, can bring positive benefits. Communications have changed enormously since this young lad delivered a Western Union telegram to a family on Long Road. In 1996, Back Office Associates was incorporated in Harwich. It is now a worldwide leader in IT communication, with additional offices around the globe.

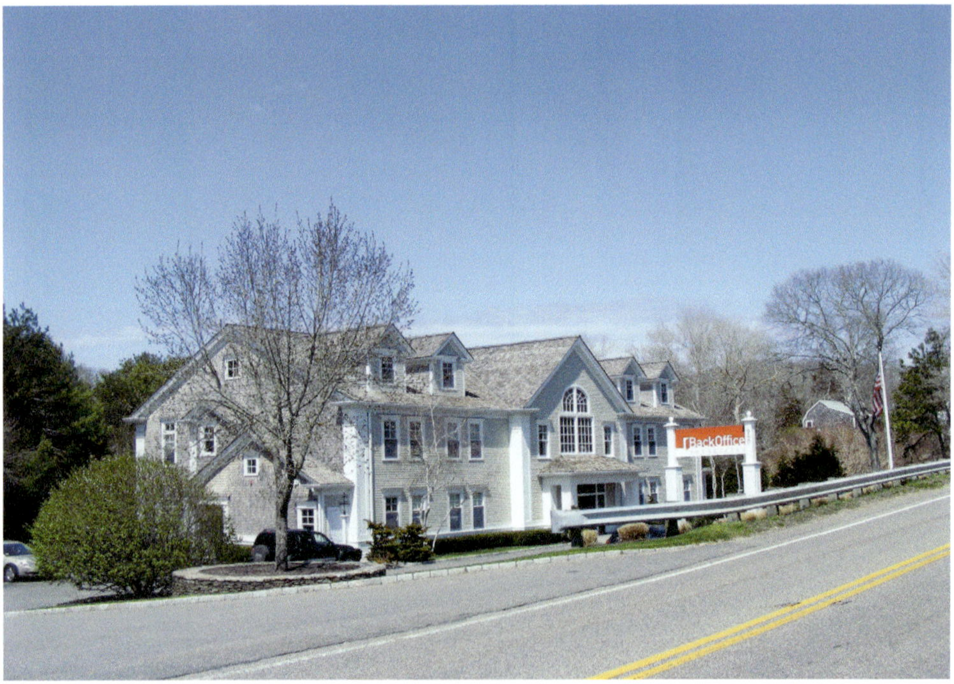

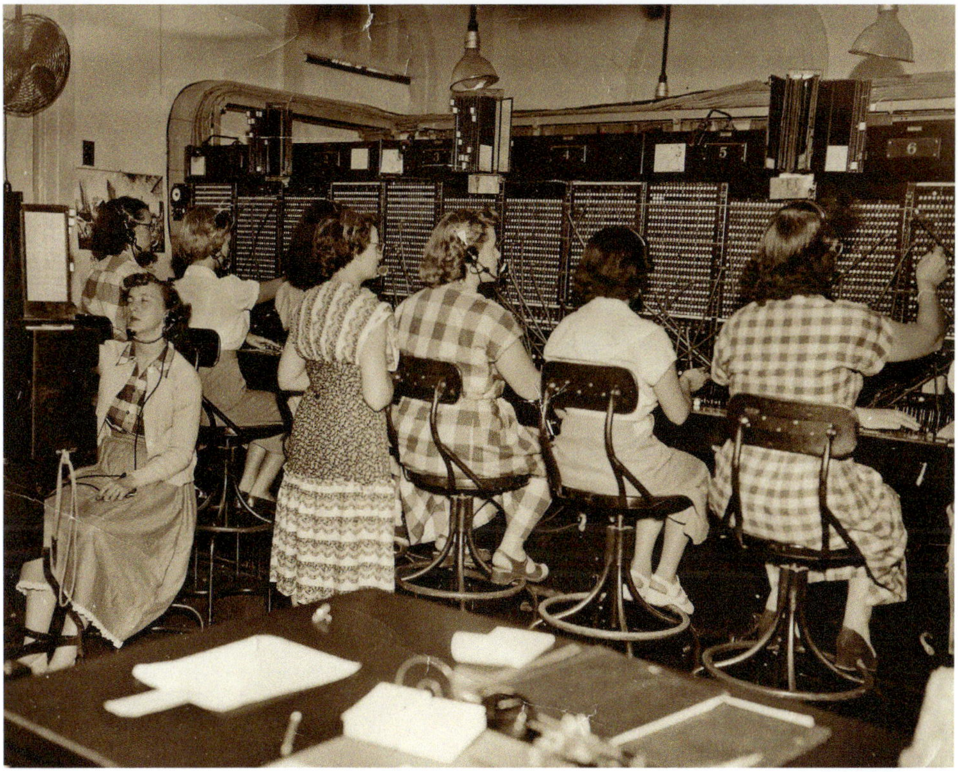

TELEPHONE TRANSFORMATIONS: It is likely that no one mourns the old crank telephone, or the operators who had to connect each call, or the neighbors who could listen in! The ubiquitous cell 'phone allows for automatic connection with almost any place in the world. This gigantic 'flag pole' adjacent to the East Harwich fire station is actually a disguised cell 'phone tower.

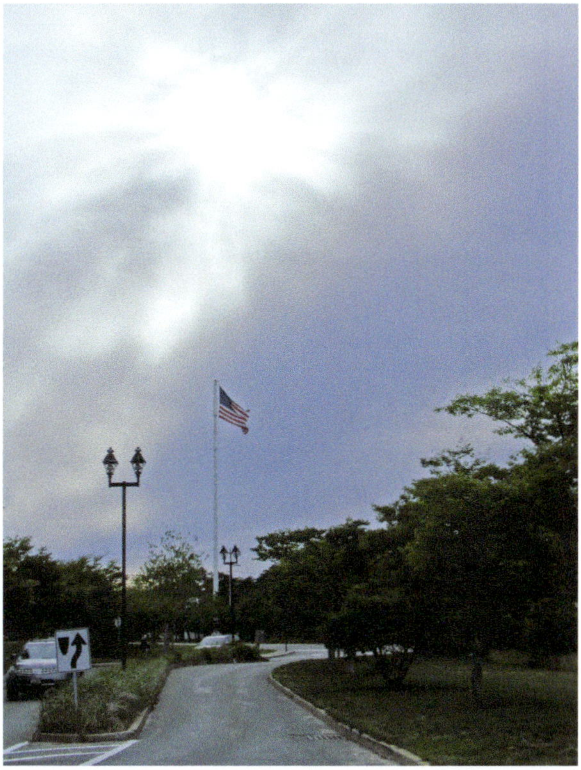

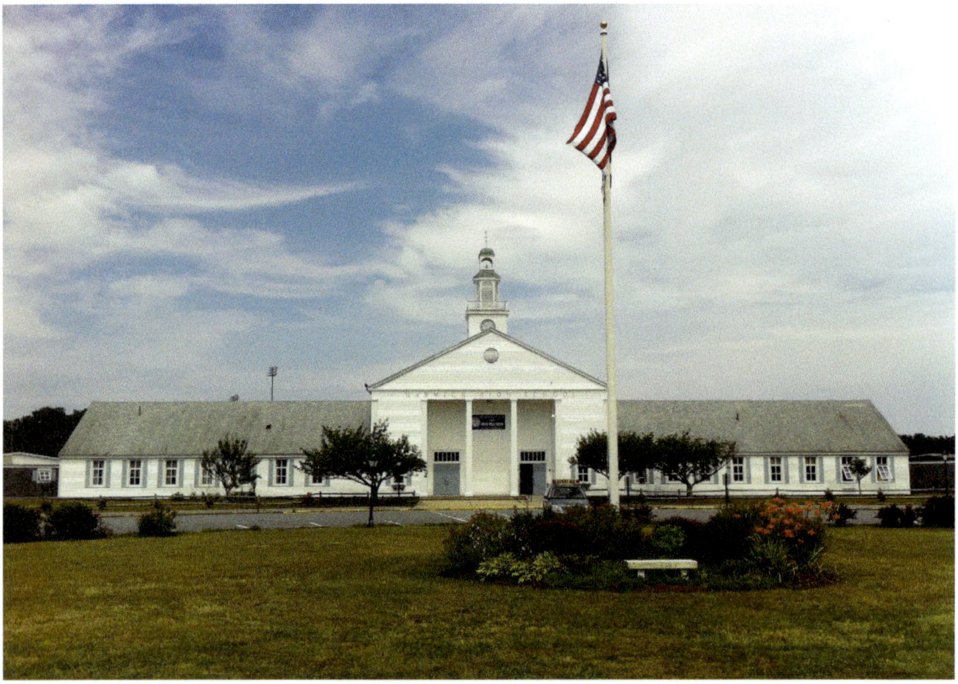

TOMORROW'S PROMISE: Harwich's faith in the future is very evident in its support of its schools. Since the first public high school opened in the 1880s, there has been a steady progression in facilities. In 2012, Chatham and Harwich voters approved a school merger that centers on construction of a new high school in Harwich with the latest educational resources. This building is being rushed to its anticipated 2014 completion, after which the present high school will be razed.

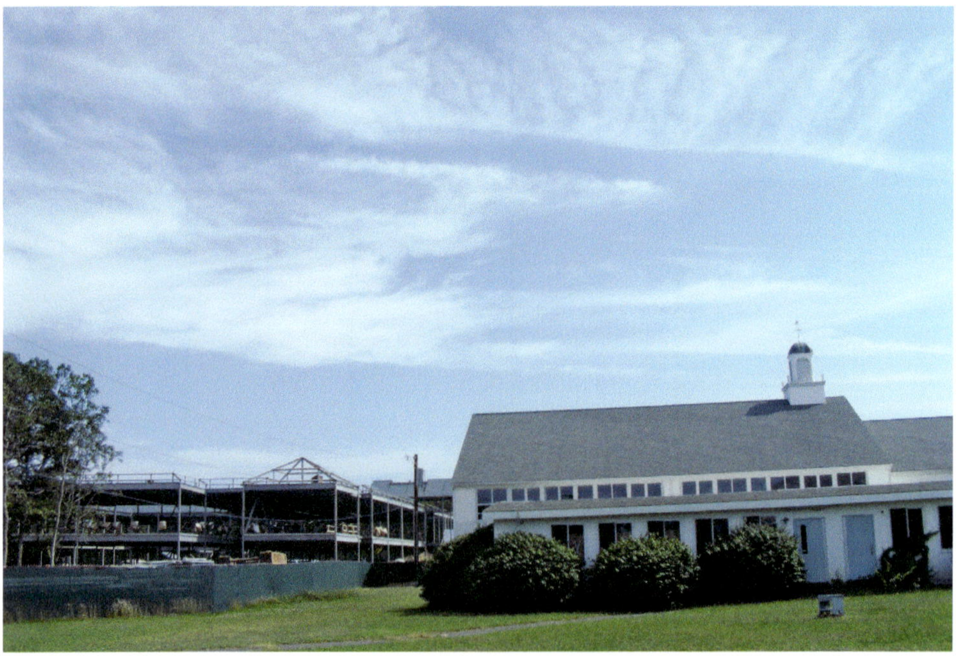

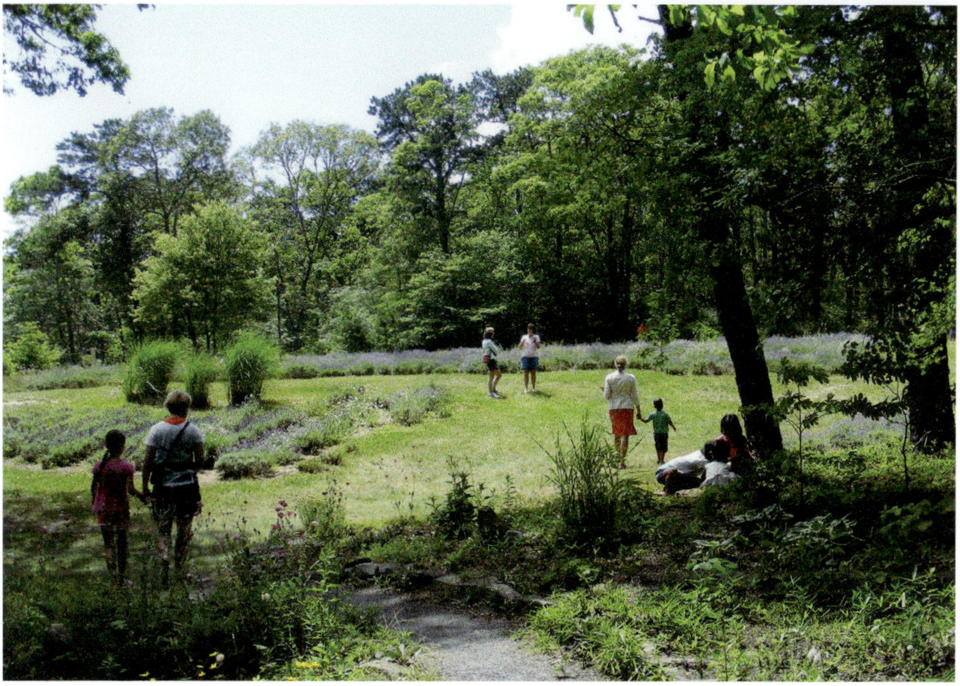

CHANGE AND ADAPTATION: When change appears inevitable, the shrewd response is to adapt. A fine example is the 12-acre Lavender Farm in Harwich Center. When the day of profitable small farming seems past, this specialty farm has become one of the largest of its kind on the east coast. It now welcomes thousands of visitors each year who delight in the plantings and innovative wee houses, and the lavender-related items in the gift shop.

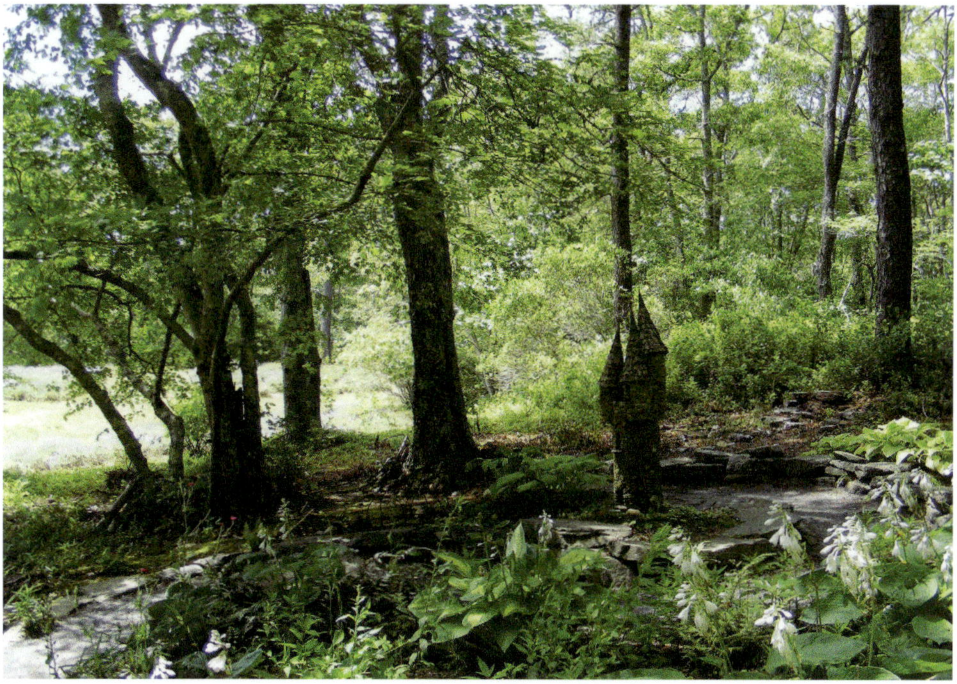

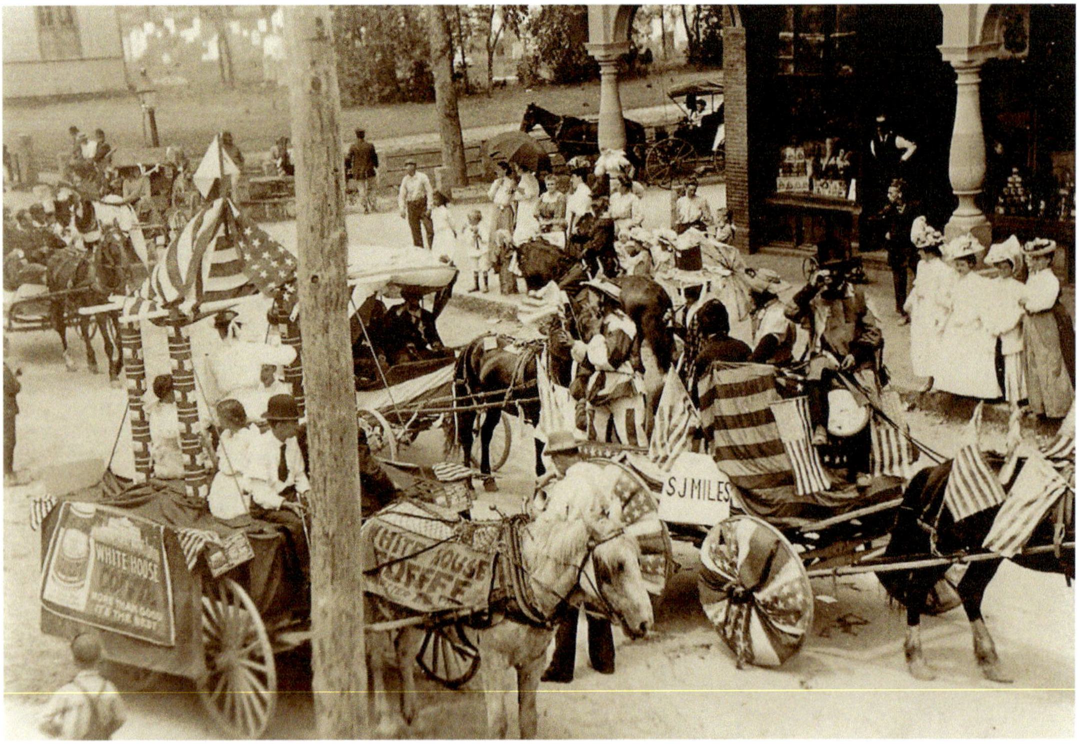

REMEMBERING THE PAST: In the midst of change, Harwich treasures its past. Since 1904 the community has staged parades to honor this past. From the delightfully attired participants of well over a century ago to the display of vintage autos, the parade is certain to bring out appreciative crowds.

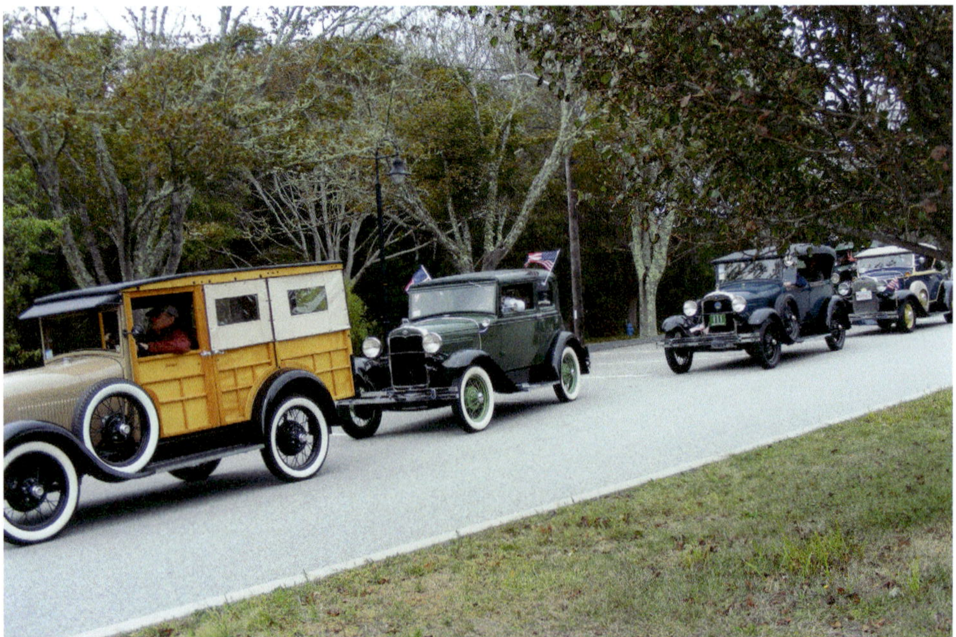

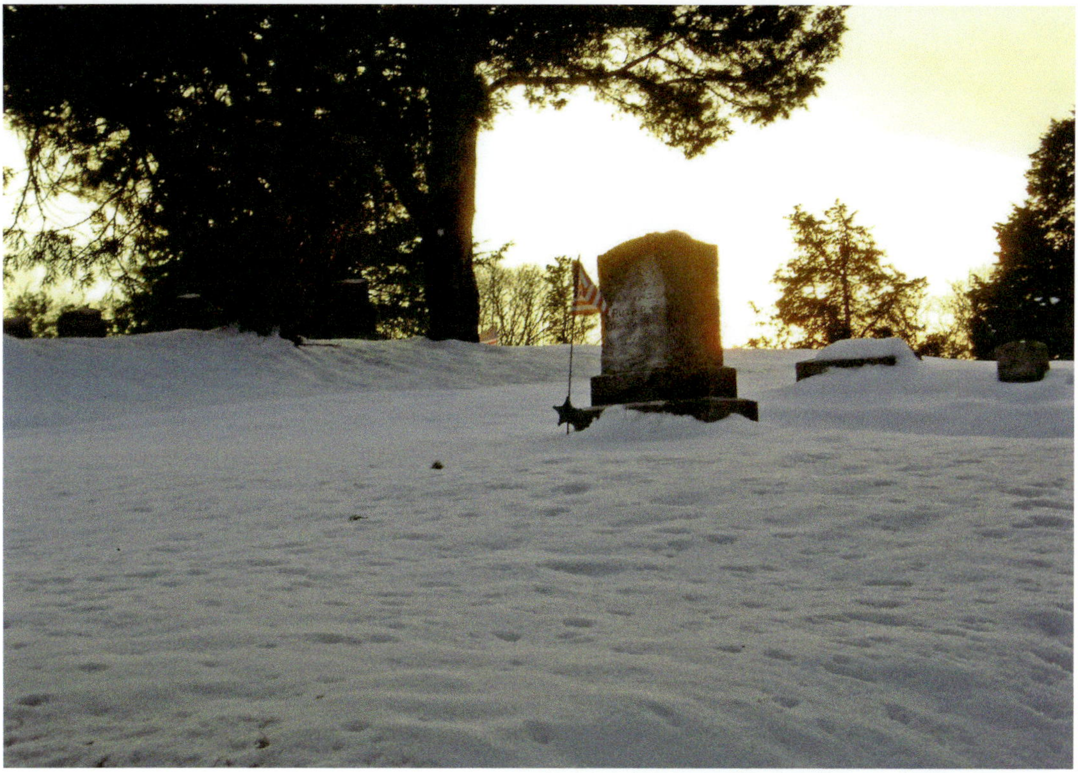

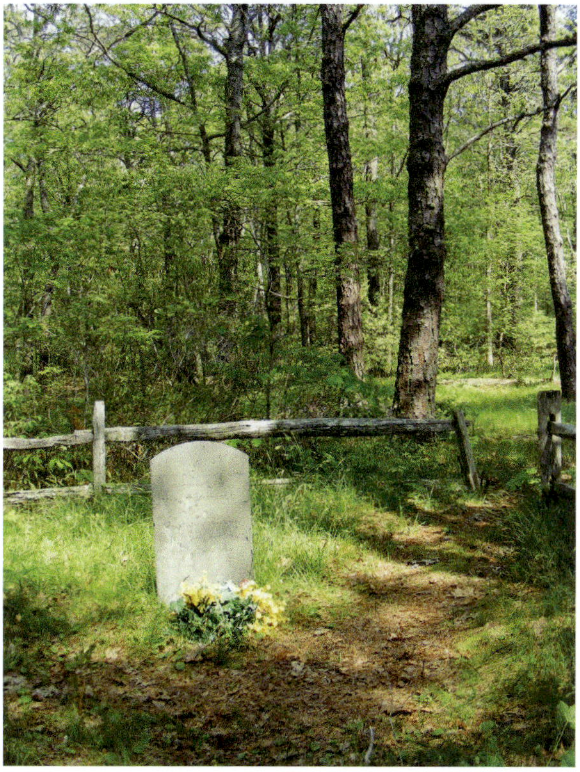

Town Cemeteries: Honoring the dead is characteristic of respect for the past. A veteran's grave of a long ago war is carefully marked with a flag in Island Pond Cemetery. Deep into conservation land, the lonely grave of a seventeen-year-old woman who in 1832 likely died in childbirth is tended by an unknown stranger.

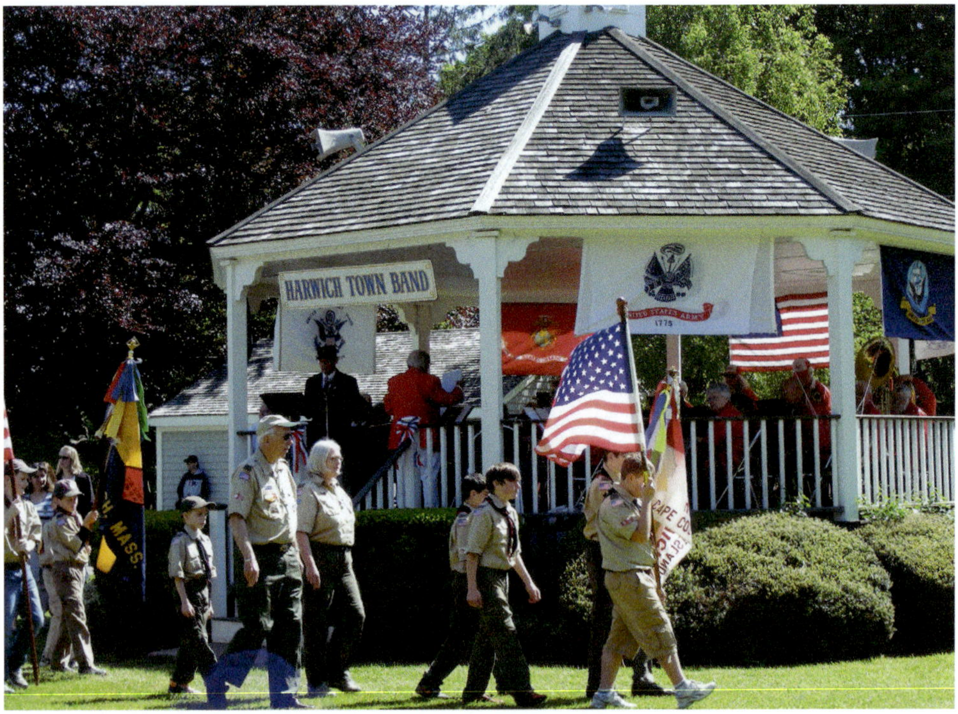

SALUTING VETERANS: In Brooks Park, to the stirring music of the town band, scouts march in honor of men and women veterans of the military. In the Congregational Church Cemetery, Civil War re-enactors salute those who fought in that war with a rifle volley. A passing civilian instinctively pauses to pay his own respect.

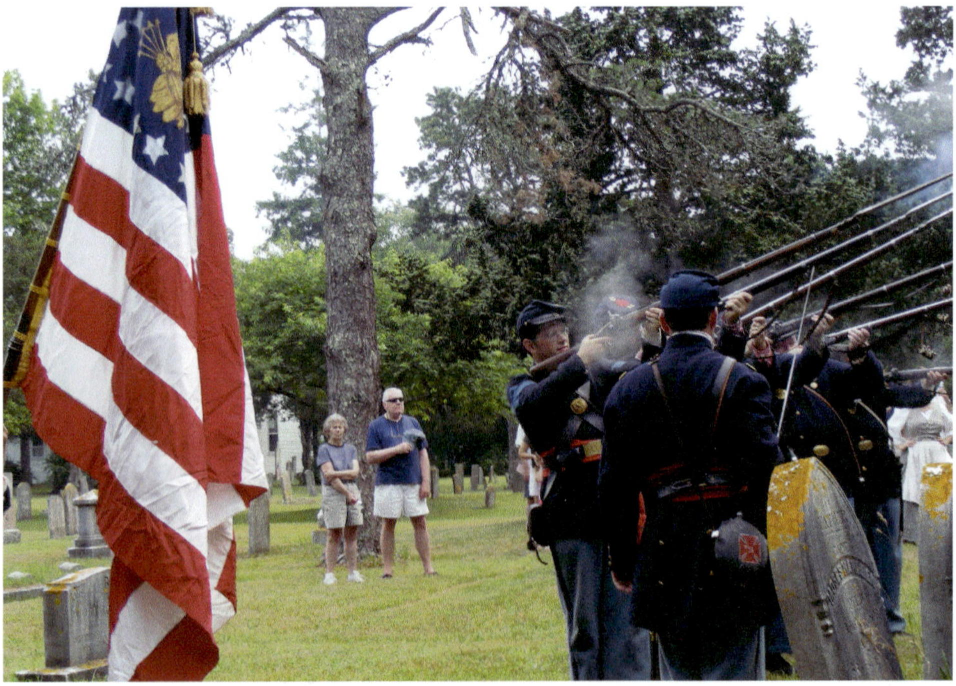